Published by PERIPLUS EDITIONS (HK) LTD.,
with editorial offices at
153 Milk Street
Boston MA 02109 and
5 Little Road #08-01
Singapore 536983.

Library of Congress Cataloging-in-Publication Data

DeMers, John, 1952–
    The food of Jamaica : authentic recipes from the jewel of the caribbean / text and recipes by John DeMers ; photography by Eduardo Fuss ; with additional contributions from Norma Benghiat.
        p. cm. — (Periplus world cookbooks)
    Includes index.
    ISBN 962-593-228-3 (hc). — ISBN 962-593-101-5 (plc.)
    1. Cookery, Jamaican. I. Benghiat, Norma. II. Title. III. Series.
TX716.J27D46 1997
641.597292—dc21   97-40523
                                                            CIP

Photo Credits:
Photos on pages 8, 9, 10, 11, 12, 14, 21, 23, 25 by Mark Downey. Photo of boats at Port Royal on page 128 by Jeremy Francis. Prints on pages 6 and 7 reproduced courtesy of Hi-Qo, Kingston. All other photos are by Eduardo Fuss. Painting on page 2 reproduced courtesy of Wolfgang Höhn. Detail on front cover from "Two Daughters" by Margaret Robson. Painting of a Jamaican scene and painting of a Jamaican kitchen on page 30 are by Fiona Godfrey.

Distributed by

USA
Charles E. Tuttle Co., Inc.
RR 1 Box 231-5
North Clarendon, VT 05759-9700
Tel.: (802) 773-8930
Fax.: (802) 773-6993

Japan
Tuttle Shokai Ltd.
21-13, Seki, Tama-ku,
Kawasaki-shi
Kanagawa-ken 214-0022, Japan
Tel.: (044) 833-0225
Fax.: (044) 822-0413

Asia-Pacific
Berkeley Books Pte. Ltd.
5 Little Road #08-01
Singapore 536983
Tel.: (65) 280-3320
Fax.: (65) 280-6290

First edition

1 3 5 7 9 10 8 6 4 2
06 05 04 03 02 01 00 99 98

PRINTED IN SINGAPORE

THE FOOD OF
JAMAICA

Authentic Recipes from the Jewel of the Caribbean

Recipes and text by John DeMers
Food photography by Eduardo Fuss
Styling by Chia Meow Huay and Christina Ong
Additional essays by Norma Benghiat
Additional photography by Mark Downey

With recipes from the following Jamaican restaurants
Ciboney
Good Hope
Grand Lido Negril
Jake's Village
Norma at the Wharfhouse
Grand Lido Sans Souci
Strawberry Hill
Terra Nova

PERIPLUS
EDITIONS

Contents

Part One: Food in Jamaica

Beneath misty mountain peaks lies
a land of infinite complexity

Jamaica is a lush tropical place offering intense adventure amid one of the most tangled cultures on the face of the earth. It vibrates with the rhythms of reggae, is enlivened by the spices of pepperpot and jerk and shimmers with the bright colors of flowers and paint.

To think of Jamaica is to picture an island paradise of steep, cloud-bedecked mountains and jewel-like blue lagoons—a land of holidays and relaxation. But there is much more to this island.

Jamaica stands out among the islands of the Caribbean for several reasons, first for its sheer size: it is the third largest island in the Caribbean. With more than 4,000 square miles, Jamaica is one of the few Caribbean islands with agriculture, thus adding depth and variety to its cuisine while liberating its people from subsisting on imported foodstuffs.

The second reason for its uniqueness is the complex ethnic makeup of its people, who were brought or came to Jamaica because of its vast tracts of tillable soil.

Today's Jamaicans are the descendants of the Amerindians, the European colonists, the African slaves, and those who came later—Germans, Irish, Indians, Chinese, Lebanese, Syrians and Arabs.

Jamaica's cuisine is the product of this diverse cultural heritage, and its food tells the story of its people. The cuisine's unique flavors include mixtures of tanginess and burning hot pepper, the rich complexity of slowly stewed brown sauces, the spice of intense curries and the cool sweetness of its many tropical fruits.

Some of the most authentic examples of the island's food are found in the most humble roadside eateries. And some of its best new fusions can be discovered in the island's hotels and restaurants, being prepared by chefs who are joining traditional flavors with new ingredients.

This book aims to unravel Jamaica's many-faceted culture and make it come alive for you. Whether you have visited often or never, these pages will cast light onto the island's history, culture and, most of all, its cuisine. The recipes offered here run the gamut of the island's offerings—from the most humble, but tasty, fried bread to its spiciest jerk chicken.

Perhaps by reading in these pages about Jamaica's history, landscape, people and food, you will begin to share the pleasures of this multilayered island paradise, which is as complicated as its stormy history and many cultures, as beautiful as its rare wildlife and flowers and as unforgettable as its easy yet knowing Caribbean smile.

Opposite:
A typical island breakfast of Run Down (recipe page 62), boiled green bananas and potatoes.

Native Soil

An Eden-like land of fertile fields and sandy beaches

From its primal beginnings, Jamaica was ripe for harvest. "The fairest land ever eyes beheld," scribbled an eager new arrival in his journal. "The mountains touch the sky." This visitor was hardly the last to be awestruck by Jamaica's beauty, but he was probably the first to write anything down. The year was 1494. The visitor was Christopher Columbus on his second voyage to the New World, and he had come to claim this "fairest land" for God, for himself, and for Spain.

Hardly a set of eyes has settled on these mountains, waterfalls and hills that roll and dive down to the palm-fringed sand, without the beholder thinking he was seeing the biblical Garden of Eden. It is important, however, to understand the interworkings of nature and man that have shaped Jamaica.

Known to Jamaica's first residents, the Arawaks, as Xaymaca (land of wood and water), the island was just that before the arrival of Europeans. It featured the two elements in its name—both important to the Arawaks and anyone else hoping to settle here—but little else except a tangle of mangroves. For all the human suffering they brought, the Spanish and British also covered the island with colorful, edible vegetation. The tropical fruits and flowers of this beautiful island are transplants from places like India, China, and Malaysia. Still, nature has been bounteous, offering its many colonists fertile fields in addition to beauty and other resources. The colonizers visited many other Caribbean islands, leaving most of them as spits of sand dotted with a few palm fronds. But in Jamaica they stayed, shaping the island to their own image.

Located in the western Caribbean, Jamaica is larger than all but Cuba and Hispaniola. Millions of years ago the island was volcanic. The mountains that soar to nearly 7,500 feet are higher than any in the eastern half of North America. These peaks run all through the center of Jamaica. The island has a narrow coastal plain, no fewer than 160 rivers and a dramatic coastline of sand coves. Much of Jamaica is limestone, which explains the profusion of

Collecting and counting bunches of bananas to fill the cargo holds of boats destined for North America. On the return trip the boats were filled with a very different sort of cargo—tourists escaping the bleak northern winter.

underground caves and offshore reefs—not to mention the safe and naturally filtered drinking water that first impressed the Arawaks. In the mountains of the east (the highest, Blue Mountain Peak, rises to 7,402 feet) misty pine forests and Northern Hemisphere flowers abound. Homes there actually have fireplaces, and sweaters are slipped on in the evenings. In places, the mountains plunge down to the coast creating dramatic cliffs. The hotter, flatter southern coast can look like an African savanna or an Indian plain, with alternating black and white beaches and rich mineral springs. There are tropical rain forests next to

A late nineteenth-century print of Muirton House and Plantation, Morant Bay.

peacefully rolling and brilliantly green countryside that, save for the occasional coconut palm, could be the south of England. It is surely one of history's quirks: many parts of Jamaica (a small place by the world's standards) resemble the larger countries from which so much of its population hails.

In the heyday of the British Empire, flowering and fruit trees were brought from Asia, the Pacific and Africa; evergreens came from Canada to turn the cool slopes green; and roses and nasturtiums came from England. The ackee, which is so popular for breakfast, came from West Africa on the slave ships. Breadfruit was first brought from Tahiti by no less a figure than Captain Bligh of the *Bounty*. Sugar

cane, bananas and citrus fruits were introduced by the Europeans.

Jamaica did send out a few treasures. One of the island's rare native fruits, the pineapple, was sent to a faraway cluster of islands known as Hawaii. Its mahogany was transplanted to Central America. There are varieties of orchids, bromeliads and ferns that are native only to Jamaica, not to mention the imported fruits like the Bombay mango that seem to flourish nowhere else in this hemisphere.

The island is clearly a paradise if you are a bird, simply based on the number of exotics that call it home. Native and migratory, these range from the tiny bee hummingbird to its long-tailed cousin the

at elevations of 2950 feet (900 meters). Rain amounts vary widely around the island, from a mere 32 inches annually in the vicinity of Kingston to more than 200 inches in the mountains in the northeast. The rainiest months are May, June, October and November with hurricane season hitting the island in the late summer and early autumn.

The Jamaican economy relies heavily on agriculture, though the island is blessed with mineral deposits of bauxite, gypsum, lead and salt—the bauxite constituting one of the largest deposits in the world. Despite its significant diversification into mining, manufacturing and tourism, the island continues to struggle against a budget deficit each year. Agriculture still employs more than 20 percent of the Jamaican population. While sugarcane is clearly the leading crop, other principal agricultural products include bananas, citrus fruits, tobacco, cacao, coffee, coconuts, corn, hay, peppers, ginger, mangoes, potatoes and arrowroot. The livestock population takes in some 300,000 cattle, 440,000 goats, and 250,000 pigs.

This is the lush backdrop to life on this Caribbean island. Of course, no profile of Jamaica would be complete without a description of its single most unforgettable resource: its people.

"doctor bird" to the mysterious solitaire with its mournful cry. Visitors to Jamaica's north coast become acquainted with the shiny black Antillean grackle known as kling-kling, as it gracefully shares their breakfast toast. And those hiking through the high mountains can catch a glimpse of *papillo homerus,* one of the world's largest butterflies. Unlike most of the population, animal or human, *papillo homerus* is a native.

A tropical climate prevails in Jamaica's coastal lowlands, with an annual mean temperature of about 80 degrees Fahrenheit (26.7 degrees Celsius). Yet the heat and humidity are moderated by northeastern trade winds that hold the average to about 72 degrees Fahrenheit (22.2 degrees Celsius)

Out of Many, One Nation

Commerce and colonialization
shape the face of a new nation

Listen closely in Jamaica and you will hear a thousand references from well beyond this Caribbean island. Jamaicans speak of places in England and in Israel—from Somerset to Siloah, Highgate to Horeb—except that these places are in Jamaica, too. And hopping aboard a bus, you will encounter Arawak place names like Liguanea, Spanish names like Oracabessa, and entirely Jamaican flips like Rest-and-Be-Thankful, Red Gal Ring and even Me-No-Sen You-No-Come.

These place names reveal the country's many influences, and, indeed, Jamaica's 2.3 million people form a spectrum of races that would give the most dedicated genealogist a migraine. Most people are black, or some shade of brown, but many have undertones of Chinese, East Indian, Middle Eastern (known on the island as Syrian, no matter their origin) and European. Five centuries after Columbus, the rainbow of natural colors in Jamaica's landscape is still vibrant. And there is no better metaphor than this rainbow for the mix of Jamaica's cultures. With its tension and its tolerance, this island is truly one of the globe's most fascinating ethnic environments.

The first of many peoples known to hit the beaches of Jamaica did so about a thousand years after the death of Christ. Amerindians paddled their canoes over from the Orinoco region of South America. Before that, there is the possibility that a more primitive group, the Ciboneys, spent some time here on their trek from Florida to other large Caribbean islands. The Arawaks, however, left their imprint on Jamaica.

When Christopher Columbus stepped ashore in 1494, the island had already served as the Arawaks' home for nearly five hundred years. They were, by all accounts, gentle folk. Their way of life included hunting, fishing, farming and dancing their way through a calendar of festivals. The Spanish, however, had other plans, forcing them into hard labor and killing the last of them within fifty years. Once they had Jamaica to themselves, the Spanish seemed to decide they didn't really want it. Their searches of the interior

Devon House, an 1881 mansion, was built by George Stiebel, a black Jamaican who made his fortune in South America. It once housed the National Gallery and is open to the public.

This Rastafarian, selling Caribbean lobster near Buff Bay, grows a beard and dreadlocks to demonstrate his pact with Jah *(God). The Rastafarian religious movement grew out of Jamaica's slave society.*

and enjoyed the protection of His Majesty's government no matter what he chose to plunder.

The notorious Port Royal (known as the Wickedest City in Christendom) grew up on a spit of land across from present-day Kingston. Morgan and his brigands found a haven there where ships could be repaired and loot could be spent. Morgan enjoyed a prosperous life. He was actually knighted and appointed lieutenant governor of Jamaica before the age of thirty. Port Royal, however, did not fare so well. On June 7, 1692, an earthquake tipped most of the city into the sea, and a tidal wave wiped out whatever was left. Port Royal disappeared. Recently, divers have turned up some of the treasure, but most of it still waits in the murky depths.

The eighteenth century was prosperous for Jamaica's sugar barons, who ruled as undisputed masters of their British plantations. The island became the largest sugar-producing colony on earth, mostly through the sweat of African slaves. Magnificent residences known as "great houses" rose above the cane fields. Fortunes built on sugar were the envy of even England's king, giving rise to the expression "rich as a West Indian planter."

Such words, of course, had little meaning for the 2 million slaves brought from Africa to Jamaica and Barbados. The slaves were cruelly used and were forbidden to speak their own languages or practice their own customs. Discipline was harsh, but the slave owners could never quite quell the spirit of rebellion that existed. Jamaica has a long history of slave uprisings and of slave violence against tyrannical planters.

For the slaves, there was also the ever-present

turned up no quick-profit precious metals, so they let the land fester in poverty for 161 years. When five thousand British soldiers and sailors appeared in Kingston harbor in 1655, the Spanish simply fled.

The next three centuries under English rule provided Jamaica with its genteel underpinnings and the rousing pirate tradition that enlivens this period of Caribbean history. British buccaneer Henry Morgan was close friends with Jamaica's governor inspiration of the Maroons, descendants of escaped slaves from Spanish days. Called *cimarrones* (runaways) by the Spaniards, these men and women lived in the mountains, defying and outwitting British troops at every turn. The Maroons drew other runaways and staged rebellions until a treaty in 1739 gave them a measure of autonomy that they retain to this day.

As it turns out, the planters proved almost as rebellious as their slaves. When the thirteen American colonies declared their independence from Britain, the Jamaica House of Assembly voted to join them. This declaration never quite took hold in world politics, but it was considered a daring gesture all the same. As with cotton in the American South, the entire sugar system proved less profitable when the slave trade was abolished in Jamaica in 1807 and slavery itself ended in 1838. The transition was peaceful compared to the Civil War that divided the United States. The planters' initial plan was to hire former slaves who knew how to handle each job. But the English quickly discovered that most free men wanted nothing more to do with plantations. So a frenzied effort was launched to attract cheap labor from abroad, initiating Jamaica's great age of immigration.

Workers came in ethnic waves over the decades. As each group rose from the lowest levels of the social system, another group had to be solicited to do the island's dirty work. Small numbers of Germans and Irish came first, then workers from India and China followed in great numbers.

A full 95 percent of Jamaica's people trace their heritage to Africa, yet most have some link or distant relative tying them to Great Britain, the Middle East, China, Portugal, Germany, South America or another island in the Caribbean. In general, these groups live together peacefully—partially because they've had to over the years to survive and partially because there has been so much intermarriage.

By the mid 1900s, a "national identity" had supplanted a British one in the hearts and minds of Jamaicans. This new identity was given official recognition on August 6, 1962, when Jamaica became an independent nation with only loose ties to the Commonwealth. On that day, the Union Jack was lowered for the last time, and the new black, green and gold Jamaican flag was lifted up.

"Out of Many, One Nation" is the motto of Jamaica, though it struggles today with the same problems that plague so many Caribbean islands. Its unity can be heard in the language of its people, which carries both words and word patterns from West African languages. And when Jamaicans speak, even in dark moments, it is with a unique lilt that makes every sentence a song.

Schoolgirls during recess in Port Antonio. While these children may look relaxed, the education system in Jamaica is very competitive, with children having to take mandatory placement exams to win spots in schools, because there are not enough places for all the children.

The Rastafarians

Reggae's hypnotic beat carries Rasta's message of protest and purity

By Norma Benghiat

The tremendous mingling of cultures in Jamaica has also led to a mingling of religions. The vast majority of Jamaicans consider themselves Christian, yet there are significant communities of Jews, Hindus, Moslems and other religions. But Rastafarianism is the religion that was born in Jamaica, and it commands a serious following on the island— along with the respect of even those Jamaicans who choose not to follow it.

Say the word "Rasta" and an image of marijuana-smoking reggae musicians comes to mind, for reggae is the most well known product of this religion, spread through the world as it has been by such famous reggae musicians as Bob Marley, who closely associated reggae with Rastafarianism.

The Rastafarian religion or movement is one of the most significant phenomenons to emerge out of Jamaica's plantation slave society. It was born out of the need to counteract the denigration of people of African descent in a society that gave little recognition to the majority of its citizens. The Rastafari-

The bright colors of these knit hats at a stand outside Ocho Rios incorporate the red and gold of the Ethiopian flag and reflect the tie that many Jamaicans feel to Africa.

ans withdrew from "Babylon" or Western society and created their own music, speech, beliefs, cooking, lifestyle, and attire.

Rastas believe in the deity of the late Ethiopian king, Haile Selassie, who is the messiah, Rastafari. They believe in repatriation to Ethiopia and consider themselves to be one of the tribes of Israel. Rastafarians believe that certain Old Testament chapters speak about Haile Selassie and Ethiopia. "Jah," or God, is seen as a black man. The Rastas see themselves as the true Hebrews, chosen by "Jah." Right-living Rastas are considered to be saints, and the others are called "brethren."

The Rastafarian religion has a code against greed, dishonesty, and exploitation. Except for the sacramental smoking of ganja (marijuana, the possession, sale and use of which are illegal in Jamaica), true Rastas are law-abiding, have strong pride in black history, a positive self-image, and strive for self-sufficiency. The Rasta lifestyle reflects these beliefs.

Some of the orthodox Rastas resemble biblical figures, bearded and garbed in long robes, carrying staffs and covering their dreadlocks in turbans. Rastas quote Leviticus 21.5: "They shall not make baldness upon their head, neither shall they shave off the corners of their beard, nor make any cuttings in their flesh" as the reason for wearing dreadlocks, which are formed by leaving hair to grow naturally without combing. The longer the dreadlocks, the longer the Rasta's devotion to the holy ways of living. Many Rastas wear dreadlocks wrapped neatly in turbans, and this is the only outward sign of their religion. They incorporate the colors of the Ethiopian flag, red, green and gold, into all kinds of clothing.

The Rastas' diet, called I-tal (which means "natural" in the Rasta language), is essentially a strict vegetarian one. They believe that man should eat only that which grows from the soil. Food should not include the dead flesh of any living animal, and pork is strictly omitted. This diet also excludes manufactured food of any kind because it contains additives, which Rastas believe cause illnesses, such as cancer. In addition, the foods they eat are grown naturally, without the use of any artificial fertilizers.

I-tal cooking uses the produce of the land—peas, beans and a variety of other vegetables, starches and fruits that are locally available. While some Rastas will eat fish, chicken and I-tal food, others will eat only I-tal food in its raw state. Ganja is often included in cooked foods, and infusions are taken for medicinal purposes. Rastas abstain from hard liquor, beer and wine. Instead they drink fruit juices that are mixed to create nonalcoholic I-tal drinks.

Some Rastas do not use silverware or plates. Instead, they eat from coconut-shell bowls and calabash bowls with their fingers. This, they say, identifies them with their African roots. Some Rastas go so far as to refuse to drink processed water and instead collect rain water to use in the preparation of their food.

"Groundlings," or gatherings, are held at specific times to celebrate the birthday of Haile Selassie or the Ethiopian Christmas and New Year. At these gatherings the *niyabinga* drums and Rastafarian music create an intense spiritual mood.

Ganja, which most likely came to Jamaica with the East Indians, plays an important role in the lives of the Rastas. Ganja is smoked in cone-shaped "spliffs" made from brown paper bags or newspaper, or in a bamboo chillum pipe that is passed around by members. The Rastas smoke the herb to inspire open conversation.

The Rastas have developed their own dialect by replacing the "me" in the Jamaican Creole language with "I and I," in order to insert a positive notion of self into their speech. For example, "me have mi table" is changed to "I and I have mi table."

Vibrant colors are the hallmark of Rastafarian art, and its influence can be seen in the works of traditional artists such as Parboosingh, as well as in ceramics, the theater and dance. The profound influence the Rastas have had on indigenous musical forms is well known, from ska to rock steady to the most significant phenomenon, reggae. The latter, with its hypnotic beat and protest lyrics, has created an artistic form that has taken on a life of its own and carried the spirit of Rastafarianism throughout the world.

From the Field to the Table

*Exotic fruits and vegetables of every color and shape
find their way into Jamaican cuisine*

By Norma Benghiat

Right:
*On her way to the
market near Port
Antonio, this
woman has stopped
to show us her
freshly picked
mangoes. The
traditional way to
carry a bundle is on
one's head.*
Opposite:
*Peddlers or
higglers, like the
one pictured, are
usually female, a
tradition that
has predominated
since it was brought
over from West
Africa during the
colonial period.*

It might have been the climate and fertility that first brought the Amerindians to Jamaica, but it was the search for gold that brought the Europeans. When this search failed, they turned to the island's other resources. There are crops that were brought to Jamaica from far away that have flourished here as in no other place.

In the days of the great plantations, many slaves were allowed to grow their own vegetables in tiny plots around their huts—though animal husbandry was, for the most part, forbidden them. There was a superstition that slaves allowed to eat red meat would develop a taste for their masters. Small-time agriculture, however, prospered in this way, producing a surplus the slaves were encouraged to sell among themselves. This produced the Jamaican tradition of Sunday as market day—a swirling scene in the center of a town, the air alive with shouts of higglers (street vendors) hawking their wares.

Jamaican markets were the social gathering place for the country folk to meet to gossip and exchange news. Both the buyers and the sellers came together to partake in this weekly event, which could be likened to a country fair.

In those days, the country folk would set out very early in the morning, or often the day before, with their donkeys laden with produce. Drays drawn by mules would create a mighty traffic jam as they weaved through the throng of people.

Inside and outside the market there would be an abundance of colorful fresh fruits and vegetables—red tomatoes, mangoes and pawpaws; purple eggplants; a green abundance of chochos and callaloo; bunches of green and ripe bananas, breadfruits and plantains—all arranged to catch the eye of the passerby.

Part of the noise and bustle were the loud cries of the higglers, who, as Martha Beckwith wrote in *Black Roadways,* "had their own musical cry which rises and falls with a peculiar inflection.

" 'Buy yu' white yam!, Buy yu' yellow yam!, Buy yu' green bananas!'

" 'Ripe pear fe breakfast—ripe pear!' "

Not many itinerant vendors are to be found in towns today. The higglers have established themselves in market stalls and now often sell on the roadsides, asking prices that are higher than those in the supermarket. The produce they carry, however, is usually of superior quality.

Today's markets have changed with the times; very rarely are donkeys and carts used for transportation. The market people now arrive via bus, truck or van. There are rarely live chickens for sale. Markets are not as vibrant as they were in the pre-supermarket days, but the market is still the place to find the widest selection of fresh produce.

Much of the vegetables and fruits in Jamaica are grown by small farmers. There are very few large fruit orchards. Instead small farmers mix their fruit trees with vegetables so that the standard Jamaican backyard is thickly planted with mangoes, limes, sweet and sour sops, ackees, sugar cane, bananas, avocados and whatever else the land will hold.

Vegetables are grown both in the cooler mountains and on the plains. The Santa Cruz area of St. Elizabeth is known as the breadbasket of Jamaica. The industrious farmers here manage to produce an abundance of food, in spite of a lack of irrigation, through heavy mulching, which helps the soil retain moisture. The largest quantities of scallions, thyme and onions are grown in this area. The mountain regions produce excellent lettuce, bok choy, cabbage, scallions and thyme.

Starches and root crops consisting of breadfruit, cassava (bitter and sweet), sweet and Irish potatoes, cocos, yams, plantains and bananas both ripe and green—the latter being eaten as a starch—are grown both in the mountains and on the plains.

The island is blessed with an astonishing variety of fruits—some indigenous, others introduced over the centuries. Summer is, of course, the most abundant season for fruits such as pineapples, mangoes, otaheiti apples, sweet and sour sops, plums, naseberries and so on.

Both dairy and beef cattle are raised in Jamaica. Beef cattle were usually bred by owners of large sugar estates and other landowners who had enough acreage of pangola grass to support the cattle. Pigs were introduced into Jamaica as early as the sixteenth century by the Spaniards and became wild in the mountains. They were notably hunted and barbecued, or "jerked," by the Maroons, using a method that was uniquely their own. Originally, goats were reared by the peasantry strictly for their milk. However, with the influx of Indian immigrants, the demand for goat meat has escalated to such an extent that this meat is often more expensive than beef. Poultry was introduced in waves to the island by the Spaniards, the English, and the Africans. Many households also raise chickens on a small scale.

Fish and crustaceans were once abundant but have become scarce owing to overfishing. They now come mainly from the Pedro Banks to the south of the island, and commercially produced pond fish now fill the demand for wild fish.

The astonishing array of ingredients available on the island has been the source of inspiration for many a newcomer to Jamaica, who, eager to re-create recipes from home, has created new dishes that are at the root of today's Jamaican cuisine.

Eating and Cooking

Goat feeds and wedding cakes—
new traditions displace the old

By Norma Benghiat

Jamaica's cuisine has changed over time, and new traditions have displaced some of the old. But eating customs and dishes exist there today that are both remnants of Jamaica's colonial history and the result of its many immigrant contributions.

One cannot say enough about the influence of immigration on the food of Jamaica. Since the English had already acquired a craving for curry in India, Indians found a ready audience for their contributions to the great Jamaican cook pot. They brought from home the technique for blending fragrant curry powders and using them to showcase local meat and fish. When traditional lamb proved hard to find, they drafted the most convenient substitute. The dish curried goat was born, turning up now and again with a side of chow mein.

The Chinese and, in smaller numbers, the Syrians and Lebanese added tremendous complexity to Jamaica's culture and cuisine. The island's very old Jewish community was joined over time by migrant Arab traders from Palestine. These groups all prepared traditional dishes from their homes—curried goat and sweet and sour pork, to name a few of the many—that have become an integral part of Jamaica's cuisine.

Eating traditions hark back to the days of Britain's control of the island. During the eighteenth century on the plantations meals were copious for the residents of the grand plantation houses. The day began with a cup of coffee, chocolate or an infusion of some local herb, all equally called "tea." Breakfast was served later in the morning, a "second breakfast" was served at noon, and dinner was served in the late afternoon or evening. Both the breakfast and "second breakfast" were substantial meals, as was dinner.

Today's Jamaican breakfast varies considerably depending on where one lives. Farmers, who rise early to tend their fields, start the day with a cup of "tea." Late in the morning they may eat a substantial breakfast of callaloo and saltfish (salted cod), ackee and saltfish accompanied with yams, roasted breadfruit, dumplings or green bananas.

Plantains, which like bananas were brought to the island by the Spanish, are eaten by the locals in a variety of ways—green or ripe, salty or sweet, fried, baked or boiled. This stuffed plantain is one of the best variations.

This festive Jamaican dinner brings together the Caribbean flavors of pineapple and pork.

Sunday breakfast of ackee and saltfish or liver and onions with johnny cakes, green bananas and bammie (a flat cassava bread) and fruit.

Dinner (sometimes called late lunch as well) is the time when family and friends gather for a more relaxed meal. Rice and peas are de rigueur for Sundays, and often at least two meats—fricasseed chicken as well as a very spicy roast beef—will be served. Fried plantains, string beans, carrots and a salad might accompany the meats, followed by a pudding, cake or fruit salad. Beverages include soft drinks, lemonade, coconut water, beers and rum or rum punch.

Christmas is the most important holiday of the year for Jamaicans. This goes back to the days of slavery when there were four seasonal holidays—Christmas, Easter or Picanny Christmas, Crop over Harvest and the Yam Festival. The Yam Festival has since disappeared, but the other three holidays are still celebrated, and celebrated well.

During the eighteenth and nineteenth centuries, Christmas consisted of three nonconsecutive days—Christmas, Boxing and New Year's Days. During this time, a temporary metamorphosis occurred in the relationship between master and slaves: the slaves assumed names of prominent whites, richly dressed (most of their savings went into dressing), and

Both country and town lunches consist of some of the favorite Jamaican dishes, such as stewed peas (which are what Jamaicans call beans); curried goat; oxtail; escoveitched fish (marinated in lime juice), brown stewed fish (pan-fried and then braised in a brown sauce seasoned with hot peppers and spices) or simply fried fish. These main dishes are usually served with rice, yams, green bananas or other starches. There might also be a satisfying soup of meats, vegetables, yams, cocos (taro, also called dasheen) and dumplings served as a one-pot meal. Dinner can include stewed beef, jerked meat, oxtail and beans, fish or fricasseed chicken.

The most important meal of every Jamaican household is the traditional Sunday dinner. This is usually eaten midafternoon after eating a bigger addressed their masters as equals. Christmas celebrations began early in the morning when a chorus of slaves visited the great house, singing "good morning to your nightcap and health to the master and mistress." After this, the slaves collected extra rations of salted meats for the three days of celebrations.

The great attraction on Boxing Day was the John Canoe Dance—which is slowly dying out—and on New Year's Day, the great procession of the Blue and Red Set Girls. Each set gave a ball, and each was represented by a king and queen. The queen and her attendants wore lavish gowns that were kept secret until the day of their appearance.

For most Jamaicans today, the idea of Christmas conjures up cool days, shopping, social gatherings, and much eating and drinking. This is the time of year when the sorrel plant, used to make the traditional red Christmas drink, is in season along with the fresh gungo (pigeon) peas used to make Christmas rice and peas. A very rich plum pudding, made from dried fruits soaked for weeks in rum and port, is a must for Christmas dinner. It is usually served with a "hard" or brandy sauce.

Easter time reflects the passing of the cooler months and heralds the coming of summer. For strict Catholics, it means the abandoning of meats for fish. Even though the majority of the Jamaican population is not Catholic, more fish is eaten during Lent than at any other time of the year.

The eating of bun and cheese during Easter is a truly Jamaican innovation. Buns of every description are baked and eaten in large quantities—especially as a snack with a piece of cheese. Each bakery vies with the next to produce the best buns. But the buns of yesteryear, most of which were baked by small bakeries, were much tastier than today's. Now the large bakeries make most of the buns, and at times the raisins and currants are hardly visible except as decorations.

Jamaican weddings today have become much like those in the United States. But of more interest were the old country weddings, celebrated grandly and often attended by the whole village. They were preceded by many nights of preparation, usually consisting of ring games. A feed was held the night before the wedding for the groom. This consisted of curried ram goat and sometimes "dip and fall back," a dish of salted shad cooked in coconut milk and served with a lot of rum. It is said that the goat's testicles were roasted and served to the groom. These days, mannish water, a stew made of a goat's organs and head is served to grooms the night before the wedding to increase virility.

The day before the wedding a procession of young girls, all dressed in white, carried the wedding cakes on their heads to the bride's house. The main cakes were in the form of pyramids, and each cake was covered with a white veil. The picturesque custom of young girls carrying the cakes on their heads has almost disappeared as transportation by cars is now used more often.

The wedding feast differed from village to village, but usually it consisted of a huge meal of roast pig, curried goat and traditional side dishes. The Sunday following the celebrations, the couple attended church with members of the wedding party.

While these traditions are slipping away, the flavors of the past are alive and well in Jamaica.

The Joys of Jerk

The island's fiery food fetish has become a global addiction

Jerk—the fiery food that is now popular throughout the globe—is truly a part of Jamaica's history. From M.G. Lewis in 1834 to Zora Neale Hurston in 1939, chroniclers of the West Indies tell us of their flavorful encounters with the Maroons—and even with the Maroons' favorite food, a spice and pepper-encrusted slow-smoked pork called "jerk." The Maroons, escaped slaves living in Jamaica's jungle interior, developed many survival techniques—but none more impressive than the way they hunted wild pigs, cleaned them between run-ins with the law, covered them with a mysterious spice paste and cooked them over an aromatic wood fire.

Lewis gives us a vivid picture of a Maroon dinner of land tortoise and barbecued pig: "two of the best and richest dishes that I ever tasted, the latter in particular, which was dressed in the true Maroon fashion being placed on a barbecue, through whose interstices the steam can ascend, filled with peppers and spices of the highest flavor, wrapped in plantain leaves and then buried in a hole filled with hot stones by whose vapor it is baked, no particle of juice being thus suffered to evaporate."

Even more exciting is Hurston's description a century later of an actual hunting expedition with the Maroons. As an anthropologist, she was trained to discern cultural and ethnic truths. But in one extended passage, what she discovers is the unforgettable flavor of jerk pork.

"All of the bones were removed, seasoned and dried over the fire to cook. Towards morning we ate our fill of jerked pork. It is more delicious than our American barbecue. It is hard to imagine anything better than pork the way the Maroons jerk it. When we had eaten all that we could, the rest was packed up with the bones and we started the long trek back to Accompong."

Thanks to Americans who have followed in Hurston's footsteps, the jerk-scented "trek back to Accompong" has never ended. The Maroon method of cooking and preserving pork has become a Jamaican national treasure, inspiring commercial

A cook serves up jerk at Faiths Pen—a lively collection of fast-food stalls along the highway that crosses the island between Ocho Rios and Kingston.

spice mixes, bottled marinades and the use of the word "jerk" around the world.

The word "jerk" itself, as with so many in Jamaica, is something of a mystery. Most Jamaicans offer the non-scholarly explanation that the word refers to the jerking motion either in turning the meat over the coals or in chopping off hunks for customers. Still, there is a more serious explanation.

"Jerk," writes F. G. Cassidy (who penned the *Dictionary of Jamaican English* published in London in 1961), "is the English form of a Spanish word of Indian origin." This process of linguistic absorption is so common in the Caribbean that it is persuasive here. Cassidy says that the original Indian word meant to prepare pork in the manner of the Quichua Indians of South America. Thus, jerking was learned from the Indians, either the Arawaks or others from across the Caribbean, and preserved by the Maroons. There's also an undeniable link to the Dutch word *gherken,* meaning "to pickle or marinate."

Until recently, jerk remained a dish made with pork, true to its roots. Now roadside pits and "jerk centers" dish up chicken, fish, shrimp—even lobster. Until recently, jerk was found only in parts of Jamaica with strong Maroon traditions, including the interior known as Cockpit Country and a tiny slice of Portland on the northeast coast at Boston Bay. Now jerk is sold everywhere, and its irresistible scent, which impressed Lewis and Hurston in their day, fills the air.

At this jerk stand in Port Antonio, near the mecca of jerk, Boston Bay, chicken is cooked over coals made from burning wood and pimento (allspice) branches. Jamaicans short on space often saw oil drums in half and build a fire on the bottom of the drum while cooking the meat on a grill above it.

Several of the best jerk purveyors are still on the beach at Boston Bay, somewhat off the tourist track and therefore frequented by Jamaicans. These eateries are little more than thatch-roofed huts built over low-lying, smoldering fires. On top of these fires you'll often find sheets of tin, blown off some roof in a storm, that are used as griddles. The meat is cooked on these sheets, covered with plantain leaves.

The jerk sellers tend to be characters with colorful nicknames and singsong sales pitches that tell you why their jerk is the best on the island. If you don't believe them, they'll pull out glass jars of their jerk paste, warn you it's lethal with Scotch Bonnet peppers, and scoop some out for a tasting on the spot. They'll even be delighted to sell you a Red Stripe to cool down your flaming taste buds.

The Spirit of Jamaica

Sugar's surprising by-product turns an indulgence into an industry

Rum, the wild firewater of slaves and buccaneers, is the spirit of Jamaica. As an industry it is more important to Jamaica's economy than sugar—even though sugar producers failed to notice its value for the longest time.

No one is certain how rum got its name, but it may be a short version of sugar's botanical name, *sac charum officinarum.* According to one story the name derives from "rumbustion" or "rumbullion," archaic English words meaning "uproar" or "rumpus."

The process of refining sugar from raw cane produces a by-product of juice and molasses. In sugar's heyday, this by-product was sometimes given to slaves or to livestock. Sometimes it was simply tossed out. Finally, someone noticed that a chemical change was occurring in the by-product. All the heat and natural yeast in the island air spontaneously brought about fermentation. According to Jamaican legend, an extremely thirsty slave dipped a ladle into a trash pool and emerged from the experience a good deal happier than he had been before. Before long, plantation owners were building distilleries alongside their sugar refineries.

By the nineteenth century, when the emancipation of slaves had made sugar less profitable, rum remained a high-profit item and was produced everywhere. There were 148 distilleries in Jamaica in 1893. Today, 4.5 million gallons of rum are produced on the island each year. Some of the best-known brands are Appleton, Gold Label and Myers.

The production of rum, then and now, involves three stages: fermentation, distillation and aging. Water and yeast are added to molasses and allowed to ferment. Distillation produces a colorless liquid: dark rums are sometimes enriched with "dunder," solid matter left in the still from previous batches.

Traditionally, Jamaican rum was stored in oak casks, for three to twenty years, depending on the type of rum and the bouquet desired. A light amber color is imparted by the oak; caramel is added to give the rum a darker color. These days, huge stainless steel vats are replacing the oak casks, and the aging process is being shortened to one to three years. Twenty-year-old rum, a rarity, is looked upon with the same esteem in Jamaica as a good cognac in France.

That said, it follows that this liquid has a special mystique around the island. It is widely imbibed for its medicinal properties, and islanders use it as a rub to treat fevers and prevent colds. Beyond that, rum is used ritually when you add a room to your house in Jamaica. You simply must sprinkle it over the area to be enclosed to ward off spirits or the dreaded evil eye.

Blue Mountain Bounty

*Jamaica's coffee leads the world in price
and pleasure by the cup*

"Blue Mountain coffee, the most delicious in the world . . ." Those words were not spoken by some highly paid spokesperson for the Jamaican coffee industry but by Agent 007 himself—world-class spy James Bond.

Bond author Ian Fleming, who lived a great part of the year in a house called Goldeneye outside Ocho Rios, no doubt developed a taste for Blue Mountain before it became the world's most expensive coffee. Actually, Bond's statement sounds a little overblown to connoisseurs of coffee, but that is strictly a matter of taste. Blue Mountain's light, almost tealike subtlety sets it apart from the more robust and full-bodied brews of Kenya or Tanzania.

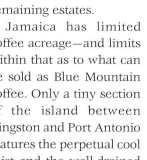

As much as it might like to be, Jamaica is not the birthplace of coffee. Louis XV sent three plants to Martinique in 1723, and only one survived the trip despite incredible pampering. Five years later, the Jamaican governor, Sir Nicholas Lawes, brought seedlings from Martinique and planted them just outside Kingston. The government supported coffee cultivation in hopes of easing the economy's dependence on sugar. The industry grew slowly, century to century, only to be virtually wiped out by a hurricane in 1951. Happily, one Victor Munn had a tiny five-acre plot at Mavis Bank in the Blue Mountain foothills. He set up a small factory and was able to process his coffee, as well as that from the few remaining estates.

Jamaica has limited coffee acreage—and limits within that as to what can be sold as Blue Mountain coffee. Only a tiny section of the island between Kingston and Port Antonio features the perpetual cool mist and the well-drained peaks of volcanic loam required to produce these beans at their best. Of Jamaica's 28,000 acres of coffee, a mere 9,000 are within the official Blue Mountain region. There, above 2,000 feet, Jamaican growers germinate their arabica seeds for one to two years, then cut off one of the two root systems before planting. It's a lengthy five years before the first harvest, yet clearly (given its price) Blue Mountain is worth the wait.

Though the many hues of these coffee beans are lovely, they are actually beans culled from the bushes; had they remained on the plant they would have interfered with the proper ripening of other beans.

The harvest itself is slow and labor-intensive. The job is done by hand: When the beans are red and at their peak of ripeness, they are picked one at a time. They are then carried down the mountain by men or mules and processed at ramshackle coffee stations that are very humble in comparison to their finished product. The beans are then sorted, and the outer pulp is removed from the inner beans, which are then dried, husked, and roasted.

In the middle of the nineteenth century, Britain instituted a new trade policy under which Jamaican coffee growers lost their protected trade status. Small Jamaican coffee growers were nearly wiped out by having to compete with coffee growers from South America.

By 1973, the coffee market had grown again to the point that some government control was required. Almost any coffee grown, processed or even vacationing in Jamaica was sold (and, of course, priced) as Blue Mountain. Yet the quality was not always there. To change this, the government issued a decree that only coffee grown in a specific region and processed by one of four estates (Mavis Bank, Silver Hill, Moy Hall and the Government Station at Wallenford) could be labeled 100 percent Blue Mountain coffee. Any other Jamaican coffee would be graded as Blended Blue Mountain (20 percent expensive beans), High Mountain Blend, or Lowland coffee.

It is the Japanese who deserve the credit, or the blame, for the fame (and high prices) of the best Blue Mountain coffee. Japanese investors bought large parcels of coffee-growing land in Jamaica in the early 1980s. This brought an infusion of money into the industry, but it is also why so much Jamaican coffee goes directly to Japan. About 80 percent of all beans from these mountains are exported there, where the coffee sells not for $15 per pound but for $15 per brewed cup. And brewed coffee is more than 99 percent water!

With the Japanese hold on the market, most Blue Mountain coffee that reaches the United States in recent years has been shipped to Japan first and then resold to buyers in the States. Markups tend to accumulate under such circumstances, as does a certain mystique. In the end, it's the law of supply and demand that pushes prices above $30 per pound, and sometimes as high as $50. Happily for growers in the Blue Mountains, there are many coffee drinkers who swear they will drink no other brew.

Left:
A worker picking beans from coffee bushes in the Blue Mountains.
Opposite:
Coffee from Mavis Bank Central Factory, an old-fashioned coffee grinder and a stunning view of the mountains from the balcony at Strawberry Hill. Mavis Bank is one of four pulperies, or processing plants, that process all beans from the Blue Mountains.

A Jamaican Dine-Around

Where to sample the best of everything Jamaican

In recent years, certain Jamaican dishes have been glorified as part of the national cuisine. Rice and peas, ackee and saltfish, and peppery jerk pork are presented now as exemplars of the flavor, the spirit and the soul of the Jamaican people.

Yet even today, crisscrossing Jamaica with eyes open and appetite engaged is a rich experience of cultural and geographic diversity. In the larger cities (and, of course, in the posh seaside resorts) it can be difficult to get beyond the modern cuisine served up for vacationing tourists. To truly taste the bounty of the real Jamaica you will have to step off the beaten track just a bit.

Right:
Norma at the Wharfhouse offers romantic seaside dining.
Opposite:
Eating breakfast on the verandah of Good Hope, one can enjoy Jamaica's flowering trees and birds.

When you take this step, you will be rewarded with the flavors of foods like jerk pork on Boston Beach near Port Antonio, mannish water cooked in a tin pot in someone's backyard, the fiery wonders of Ugly Man's (hot) Pepper Farm and peanut root tonic.

Beginning in Montego Bay, the roads that lead around the island offer a wealth of discoveries. In a suburb of MoBay (Montego Bay to the uninitiated) chef Norma Shirley keeps her kitchen humming in a romantic waterfront setting. If you want the cutting edge of Caribbean cuisine and true Jamaican flavors, check out **Norma at the Wharfhouse** (locally called **Norma's**).

Heading east, there are the resorts of the north coast between MoBay and Ocho Rios. Today, most of the best ones operate as "all-you-can-eat" affairs. The food in these places (especially resorts like **Half Moon Bay**, **Sans Souci** and **Ciboney**) has become much more interesting as visitors seem more and more interested in tasting Jamaican cuisine. Getting your smoked marlin, ackee and saltfish or rice and peas from a buffet table may not be the most traditional encounter with Jamaica, but it has to be one of the most pleasurable when it is merely footsteps from the sea.

Sans Souci, part of the elegant Lido collection of resorts, has come into its own in recent years, serving up some of the classiest New World Meets

Jamaican dishes anywhere. A somewhat more traditional approach is taken at **Ciboney**, where the chefs work wonders with fresh local ingredients. And if you're visiting Noel Coward's mountaintop retreat at **Firefly**, you can dine on simple local foods while gazing awestruck down at the curving coast.

At Port Antonio, Errol Flynn's old hangout and the birthplace of Jamaica's tourism, you can taste I-tal cooking, the vegetarian cuisine of the Rastafarians. From breakfast at the **Town Talk** (boiled green bananas, callaloo and a breadfruit dumpling) to lunch at **Sister Fire's Garden of Eating** at Fairy Hill Beach (vegetable run down burning with Scotch bonnet peppers), there is much to recommend Rasta cooking.

If you journey across the Blue Mountains you can sample Blue Mountain coffee at the processing station of **Mavis Bank** and Dr. Ian Sangster's marvelous rum liqueurs at **World's End**.

The famous food stop of any cross-mountain trip is an exotic little place known as **Faiths Pen**. Approximately halfway between Ocho Rios and Kingston, this curve in the road has fast food as few have experienced it: stall after stall with names like **Johnny Cool Number 1**, **Sparrow's One Stop** and **Shortie's Place**. Everything that can be jerked in a smoke-filled converted oil drum is jerked at Faith's Pen, along with unbelievable corn that is slathered with crushed Scotch bonnets.

Strawberry Hill in the Blue Mountains takes a creative and mostly modern approach to traditional food, doing intriguing things with curries and fresh tropical fruits. Kingston itself offers up some fine dining opportunities, led by the restaurant at the

The vibrant paintings in the dining room at Jake's village give the place a festive atmosphere. The tables were painted by Jamaican artist Ritula Frankel.

Terra Nova Hotel. After spending some time in Kingston—tramping through the Constant Spring Market, tasting vegetable patties at **Mother's**, dining outside on fried fish at **The Fish Place**—it's time to head west along the road less traveled to Jamaica's southern coast.

On the south coast near the Black River, the island's freshwater seafood and saltwater favorites, can be sampled at the bohemian **Jake's** resort.

Worthwhile stops include sampling fish from the "fish ladies" at Old Harbour and getting a lesson in making bammies (thick pancakes of grated cassava) from Joy Manson at the Pickapeppa and ackee factories near Mandeville, plus a lunch at the curry goat stands on Spur Tree Hill Road. Don't miss the mannish water on the road to Black River—at Parotee Point, to be precise.

In a tiny village called Middle Quarters you should taste the orange-red food you've seen sold in plastic bags by ladies on the side of the road. It's pepper shrimp—freshwater shrimp boiled in salty brine that's been spiked with Scotch bonnet peppers.

A final rite of passage before heading north to Montego Bay is the fishing village turned bohemian paradise of Negril. By far the classiest place to dine around Negril is the **Grand Lido** resort.

Almost everything Jamaican can be sampled in and around Negril. With the large number of young people enjoying Negril's night life at places like **Cheap Eats**, **De Buss** and **Alfred's Ocean Palace**, you shouldn't be surprised to find that hamburgers are the "national dish" in these parts. But in Jamaica's cross-cultural spirit at least some of them come dressed with delicious mango chutney.

Fiona M. Godfrey '97

Part Two: The Jamaican Kitchen

From traditional to modern,
this kitchen serves up simple and celebratory food

There are Jamaican kitchens so traditional that they seem like historic re-creations—and others so modern they look no different from those found in the United States or Europe. In between these extremes, with modernization based primarily on income, most Jamaicans prepare their meals using a combination of old and new implements.

Visiting the island's plantation great houses one spots the most time-honored elements of the Jamaican kitchen. Old-fashioned cooks still use the African **yabba**, an earthenware pot that's perfect for slow cooking, a **calabash**, which is a gourd used as a container, and the **kreng kreng**, a basket or wine container in which meat or fish can be smoked over an open fire. In some areas, huge wooden **mortars** are still used for pounding corn, plantain or yam, even though several more modern implements are also available.

To outfit the Jamaican kitchen today, or indeed to prepare authentic Jamaican food in kitchens around the world, requires little more than the standard equipment most people have already.

In the preparatory phase of any island recipe, there are a few utensils that speed things along. The simple, inexpensive **mortar and pestle** comes in handy, if not for large jobs like pounding corn at least for small ones like grinding spices. A **blender, electric grinder** or **food processor** can also be used. Just be sure that you know the consistency of what you are trying to produce, then experiment until the finished product looks right. Younger cooks are also adopting the use of the **rice cooker**, which is quite a time saver.

The two most basic cooking vessels in the Jamaican kitchen are a heavy (traditionally cast-iron) **skillet** for the many dishes that require frying and a **large soup pot**, **kettle** or **Dutch oven** for those that need slow cooking.

For grilling or jerking meat, you will not need the misshapen and pock-marked 50-gallon oil drum that's most commonly used. **Gas grills** and **smokers** work just as well and do entirely acceptable jobs on Jamaican recipes that call for this cooking method.

Finally, for turning and lifting foods as they cook you can't do without a high-handled frying **spatula** and a **circular perforated ladle**. These come in different shapes and sizes, but you really need only one of each.

Left:
These earthenware yabba pots are still used in some traditional Jamaican kitchens.
Below:
This Jamaican monkey jar was used for storing and carrying water. Its design combines elements of both European and African pottery.

Cooking Methods

Mastering a few basic techniques
for cooking authentic dishes

Like the slaves in the American South, the slaves and free Africans who formed the backbone of Jamaica's population faced mealtime with little prospect of quality, variety or freshness in their food. For quality and freshness they substituted the traditional cooking methods of the poor—frying, smothering and stewing—to make inexpensive meat savory.

For variety, however, they took spicing to a different level, borrowing first from the French and Spanish, then from the Indians and Chinese. The same dreary ingredients, these early Jamaicans learned, could be turned into lively meals with the creative use of spices.

Fried foods find particular favor in Jamaica. From Escoveitched Fish to the dozens of different fritters made with conch, saltfish or beans, crispy, well-seasoned foods are dear to the Jamaican heart. While health concerns about fried food are unlikely to go away, Jamaicans stress that eating them in moderation and frying them at the proper temperature to reduce oil absorption cuts fat and cholesterol considerably.

Second to frying as a cooking technique in the Jamaican kitchen is any variation on stewing.

Whatever the island cook chooses to call his version, it's slow cooking that makes tough meat tender and bland food flavorful. The notion that a little bit of meat goes a long way to season vegetables is a basic premise of many delicious Jamaican dishes.

Surprisingly perhaps, there are many hot and hearty soups on the Jamaican menu that are prepared like every other slow-cooked dish, only with more water or stock. With the coming of professional chefs, the separate process of making stock has become part of Jamaican cuisine. Traditionally, though, the cook simply put all his or her ingredients into a big kettle, covered them with water and simmered them until they tasted terrific.

Other favored cooking methods include boiling, particularly of plantains and yams, and baking, especially of bananas and breadfruit. Grilling, of course, is common. Additional flavor is supplied to meats and vegetables alike by marinating, stuffing, and rubbing them with spices.

Above: Cast-iron cooking pots that were used for slow cooking were made in the foundries of Great Britain and brought to the colonies in the late eighteenth century.
Right: Wooden mortar and pestles were either hand turned or made by hollowing out a log or a piece of wood. In the Jamaican kitchen they were used to pound coffee, spices and even breadfruit.

Jamaican Ingredients

*A guide to unusual products
found in the Jamaican pantry*

ACKEE: A handful of islands grow ackee as an ornamental tree, but only Jamaica looks at it as a tree that bears edible fruit. The ackee fruit is bright red. When ripe it bursts open to reveal three large black seeds and bright yellow flesh that is popular as a breakfast food throughout Jamaica. Ackee's scientific name, *blighia sapida,* comes from Captain Bligh, who introduced the plant to Jamaica from West Africa. Ackee is poisonous if eaten before it is fully mature and because of its toxicity, it is subject to import restrictions and may be hard to obtain in some countries. Never open an ackee pod; it will open itself when it ceases to be deadly. Ackee is sold canned in West Indian markets.

ALLSPICE BERRY: see *Pimento.*

ANNATTO: This slightly musky-flavored reddish yellow spice, ground from the seeds of a flowering tree, is native to the West Indies and the Latin tropics. Islanders store their annatto seeds in oil—giving the oil a beautiful color. Saffron or turmeric can be substituted.

BLUE MARLIN: Jamaicans have little need for imported smoked salmon, as they enjoy their own classy variation from the nearby waters of the Gulf Stream. There's even a world-famous marlin tournament held in Port Antonio each year. The marlin that isn't immediately devoured as steaks is carried off to the smoker, where it takes on a milder salmon-like flavor and texture that holds up well when thinly sliced.

BREADFRUIT: Breadfruit was also introduced to Jamaica from its native Tahiti in 1793 by the infamous Captain Bligh. The breadfruit is a large green fruit, usually about 10 inches in diameter, with a pebbly green skin and potato-like flesh. Breadfruit are not edible until they are cooked and they can be used in place of any starchy vegetable, rice or pasta. Breadfruit is picked and eaten before it ripens and is typically served like squash—baked, grilled, fried, boiled or roasted after being stuffed with meat. It's even been known to turn up in preserves or in a beverage.

CALLALOO: Spelled half a dozen different ways, this colorful word turns up in Jamaican records as early as 1696. This leafy, spinach-like vegetable is typically prepared as one would prepare turnip or collard greens. This variety of callaloo (*Amaranthus viridis*), better known as Chinese spinach or Indian kale, should not be confused with the callaloo

Ackee

Breadfruit

Callaloo

Cho-cho

Coconut

Dasheen

Limes

found in the eastern Caribbean, which refers to the leaves of the dasheen plant.

CASSAVA: This tuber is also known as manioc and yuca. A rather large root vegetable with a 6- to 12-inch length and 2- to 3-inch diameter, cassava has a tough brown skin with a very firm white flesh. Both kinds of cassava can appear as meal, tapioca and farina and can be bought ready made as cassava or manioc meal, which is used to make bammie. Sweet cassava is boiled and eaten as a starchy vegetable. Bitter cassava contains a poisonous acid that can be deadly and must be processed before it can be eaten. This is done by boiling the root in water for at least 45 minutes (discard the water). Alternatively, grate the cassava and place it in a muslin cloth, then squeeze out as much of the acid as possible before cooking. Bitter cassava is used commercially but is not sold unprocessed in some countries.

CHO-CHO: This pear-shaped, light green, delicately flavored tropical squash, which grows on a vine, is also known as chayote, christophene and mirliton. Though most often eaten as a vegetable, cho-cho was traditionally substituted for the apples in American apple pie recipes by the Jamaicans. Zucchini can be substituted for cho-cho in most recipes, producing a more lightly flavored dish.

COCONUT: This member of the palm family, which is native to Malaysia, yields fruit all year long. Coconut is edible in both its green and mature forms. Both the water and the "jelly" of the green coconut find their way into island drinks, and meat from the mature coconut gives desserts a Caribbean identity.

CONCH: These gastropods are a beloved part of the cuisine as far north as the Bahamas and Florida. When preparing conch soup, conch salad or, best of all, spicy conch fritters, you must beat the tough conch flesh into tender submission with a mallet, the flat of a cleaver or a wooden pestle before cooking. The job can sometimes (depending on the recipe) be made easier by using a food processor.

DASHEEN: Also known as coco, taro and tannia, dasheen is a starchy tuber that is usually served boiled or cut up and used as a thickener in hearty soups. While considered by some to have a texture and flavor superior to that of a Jerusalem artichoke or potato, potatoes can often be used as a substitute for dasheen in recipes. Dasheen is often called coco, but coco is actually a slightly smaller relative of dasheen.

GOAT: Goat meat is eaten with enthusiasm in only a few places in the world, and Jamaica is assuredly one of those places. Some credit immigrants from India who searched in vain for lamb to prepare their beloved curry. Finding no lambs, they latched onto the next best thing—and curried goat became a Caribbean classic. Most first-timers find goat milder in flavor than lamb and an excellent substitute for lamb in most recipes. Of course, if you can't find goat, you can substitute lamb.

GUAVA: The Caribbean guavas are small fruits with pink seed-filled flesh. Guavas grow all over Jamaica and the fruit lends itself well to jellies, preserves, fruit cups, sauces, cocktails and desserts. Guava is also delicious when eaten raw. When green, guavas are slightly tart; when ripe, they are sweeter.

JACK: A fish family of over two hundred species, these colorful saltwater fish go by a host of varietal names such as yellowtail, greenback, burnfin, black and amber jack. These delicately flavored fish tend to be large, weighing as much as 150 pounds, and readily available in waters around the world. Tuna and swordfish make good substitutes.

LIMES: Caribbean limes have light yellow skins when ripe, though they are often picked green because they go bad rapidly when ripe. When overripe, they turn yellow and are an excellent source of vitamin C. For this reason, the popularity of these citrus fruits grew with the realization by the British Navy that they cured scurvy. Now limes are one of the most important ingredients in Jamaican sauces and marinades, and are used to perk up dishes from savory to sweet. Chicken and fish turn glorious with a mere squeeze of lime. And beverages, cakes and preserves wouldn't taste the same without it.

LOBSTER: In Jamaica, it's the spiny or Caribbean lobster that is found—the same delicious crustacean as the *langouste* in France, the *aragosta* in Italy, and the *langoasta* in Spain. Although the texture of this cooked meat is considered by some to be inferior to that of the Maine lobster, the flavor of the spiny lobster meat more than makes up for the inferior texture.

MAMMEY APPLE: This large tropical fruit, native to the New World, yields edible pulp that's tangerine in color. With a flavor similar to that of the peach, mammey turns up most often as jam.

Mammey Apple

MANGO: Actually a native of India, this fruit has come to be known as "the fruit of the tropics." Mangoes are used in a variety of ways in the Caribbean. Green mangoes are used in hot sauces and condiments, while ripe mangoes appear in desserts and candies and in drinks. The best varieties of mango are the Bombay, East Indian, St. Julian and Hayden.

Mango

NUTMEG: Jamaican cooks are insistent—when cooking their recipes, skip over the pre-ground nutmeg sold in supermarkets and buy the spice whole, grating it only as needed. Nutmeg, the inner kernel of the fruit, is more flavorful when freshly grated. The spicy sweet flavor of this aromatic spice makes it an excellent addition to cakes, puddings and drinks.

Nutmeg

OTAHEITI APPLE: Yet another fruit introduced from the Pacific by Captain Bligh, the pear-shaped otaheiti apple ranges from pink to ruby red in color. This fruit is usually eaten fresh, though it can be poached in red wine or turned into a refreshing cold drink.

PAPAYA: This native of South America is still called "pawpaw" by some Jamaicans. The papaya has an orange color when ripe, and its bland flavor resembles that of a summer squash, making it a nice complement to the

Otaheite Apple

Papaya

Peas (mixed)

Pimento

West Indian Pumpkin

sharper flavors of other fruits. Green papaya is often used as an ingredient in chutney or relishes and makes a nice main dish when stuffed. When ripe, it is eaten as a melon, or served in fruit salad. Papaya juice makes a nice drink when sweetened with condensed milk or sugar.

PEAS: Jamaicans refer to nearly all beans as "peas." Kidney beans are probably the most popular. Gungo (pigeon) peas have also been a hit since their introduction from West Africa by the Spanish, as have cow peas, black-eyed peas, and butter, lima and broad (also called fava) beans. They are the island's primary source of protein—even more than meat. Smaller peas are used in Rice and Peas while larger-sized peas often appear in savory stews and side dishes.

PIMENTO: Just to keep things interesting, Jamaicans call what the world knows as allspice "pimento"—a word that elsewhere refers to bell peppers or chiles. The more global name refers to the allspice berry, which has the taste of nutmeg, cinnamon, black pepper and clove. All the same, Jamaicans deserve a big say in this naming, since all but a tiny bit of pimento is grown in Jamaica, the remainder being grown in southern Cuba. Thanks to its embrace by English and Spanish colonists, allspice is used in numerous Jamaican classics, from Escoveitched Fish to Jerk Pork.

PICKAPEPPA SAUCE: This bottled sauce is a key ingredient in Jamaican cuisine. The sweet, sour and spicy mixture was developed by Jamaican Norman Nash in the early 1920s. It contains a combination of tomatoes, onions, cane vinegar, mango, raisins, tamarind, peppers and secret spices that is aged in oak for one year.

PLANTAIN: Vegetables! That's what plantains (which look like oversized bananas) really are, no matter how much we think of them as a fruit. Sometimes referred to as cooking bananas, plantains are starchier than bananas and should never be eaten raw. The ripe ones are especially good when fried and served as a tropical side dish.

SALTFISH: Saltfish is any dried, salted fish, but most often cod. With the increasing availability of fresh fish all over Jamaica, some cooks are moving away from this preserved fish dating back to the days before refrigeration. Still, Jamaicans have a soft place in their hearts for the taste of this salted cod (sold around the world in Italian, Spanish or Portuguese markets under some variant on the name *bacalao*). Ackee and Saltfish is the preferred breakfast of Jamaicans. When imported saltfish has been unavailable, Jamaicans have been known to make their own from fresh fish.

SCOTCH BONNET PEPPERS: The fiery Scotch bonnet pepper, ranging in color from yellow to orange to red, is considered the leading hot pepper in Jamaica, though several other varieties have recently been developed. Some peppers are sold whole, others are dried and ground, and still others are processed into sauces, such as Jamaica Hell

Fire. If you can't get your hands (wash them afterward!) on Scotch bonnets, you can substitute habaneros or jalapeños.

SORREL: Brought from India by way of Malaysia, this unusual plant was introduced to Jamaica by the British soon after 1655. Also known as roselle and, appealingly, flor de Jamaica, sorrel always blooms in December, when its deep red flower becomes an unrivaled floral decoration for two to three weeks before it evolves into Jamaica's traditional holiday beverage. At that time, the flowers are dried and then steeped in water to make a bright red drink that has a slightly tart taste and is the color of cranberry juice.

SOURSOP: Notable for the spikes all over its green skin, this fruit has a perfumed flesh that's great in drinks or ice cream. Jamaicans believe soursop soothes the nerves.

SOY SAUCE (DARK OR BLACK): Soy sauce, also called soya sauce, became available in Jamaica at the end of the nineteenth century. It adds a salty depth to many Jamaican dishes. Dark soy sauce is sweeter and less salty than light soy and has caramel added to it. Black soy is darkened with molasses.

STAR APPLE: An important part of a traditional dessert known as matrimony, the star apple is a succulent round fruit about the size of an orange. Native to Jamaica and the Greater Antilles, the skin of this fruit is either a shiny purple color or a less eye-catching green. No matter what color, the flesh of the star apple is delicious.

STINKING TOE: Actually a pod that resembles a human toe, this bizarre fruit possesses an evil-smelling and rough exterior. The sugary powder inside can be devoured on the spot or turned into a flavorful custard or beverage.

SWEETSOP: An interesting challenge to eat, the flesh of the sweetsop is actually a collection of black seeds surrounded by sweet white pulp. The sweetsop is native to the tropical Americas.

TAMARIND: This decorative tree produces brown pods containing a sweet and tangy pulp that's used for flavoring everything from beverages to curries and sauces—including Angostura bitters and Pickapeppa sauce. It is also an important ingredient in Jamaican folk medicine.

WEST INDIAN PUMPKIN: A member of the gourd, squash and melon family, this squash is also known as *calabaza*. Possessing a sweet flavor similar to that of butternut squash, this firm-textured vegetable is commonly found in soups, stews, breads and sweetened puddings. Though hardly the same, the best substitutes for calabaza are Hubbard, butternut and acorn squash.

YAM: It's important never to confuse the tuberous roots known as yams in Jamaica with the sweet potatoes grown in the United States. Surprisingly, the true yam is not related to the sweet potato. The island's three favorite varieties of yams are white, yellow and yampee—all three are delicious either boiled or roasted.

Scotch Bonnet Peppers

Stinking Toe

Soursop

Yam

Part Three: The Recipes

Basic recipes

Chicken Stock ②②

1 chicken carcass
2 medium carrots, quartered
2 medium onions, quartered
3 celery stalks, coarsely chopped
2 leeks, coarsely chopped
2 garlic cloves, crushed
2 shallots, peeled and sliced
5 parsley sprigs
2 bay leaves
1 tablespoon freshly ground black pepper
2 teaspoons salt
1 cup dry white wine
4 quarts cold water

In a large stockpot, combine all ingredients and bring to a boil, skimming off froth as it rises to the surface. Reduce the heat and simmer partially covered for at least 4 hours. Make sure stock does not boil. Remove all of the bones and strain stock through a sieve. Skim off as much fat as possible. Makes about 2 quarts.

Beef Stock ②②

1 pound beef shanks, in pieces
3 pounds beef soup bones
2 medium carrots, quartered
2 medium onions, quartered
3 celery stalks, coarsely chopped
2 leeks, coarsely chopped
2 garlic cloves, crushed

5 parsley sprigs
2 bay leaves
1 tablespoon freshly ground black pepper
2 teaspoons salt
1 cup dry white wine
4 quarts cold water

In a large stockpot, combine all ingredients and bring them to a boil, skimming off froth as it rises to the surface. Reduce the heat and simmer partially covered for at least 4 hours. Make sure the stock does not boil. Remove all of the bones and strain the stock through a sieve. Skim off as much fat as possible.

Red Stripe Chicken (left) and Soy Ginger Chicken (page 124) in the peaceful/picturesque courtyard at Jake's Village.

Time Estimates

Time estimates are for preparation only (excluding cooking) and are based on the assumption that a food processor or blender will be used.

② quick and very easy to prepare

②② relatively easy; 15 to 30 minutes' preparation

②②② takes more than 30 minutes to prepare

Fish Stock ⏱⏱

2 pounds fish bones, rinsed
2 medium onions, quartered
½ leek, chopped
½ bunch celery, chopped
½ teaspoon dried leaf thyme
1 bay leaf
1 teaspoon freshly ground black pepper
1 cup dry white wine

In a large stockpot, combine all ingredients, cover with water, and bring to a boil. Reduce the heat and simmer until the volume is reduced by half, about 1 hour. Remove from the heat, skim, and cool. Strain through a sieve before using. Makes about 1 quart.

Curry Powder ⏱

4 teaspoons ground coriander
4 teaspoons ground turmeric
4 teaspoons ground ginger
4 teaspoons freshly ground black pepper
1 teaspoon ground cardamom
1 teaspoon ground cinnamon
1 teaspoon ground fenugreek

Mix all ingredients together. Store in an airtight jar. Makes about 6 tablespoons.

Coconut Milk ⏱⏱

1 large mature coconut, without cracks and
containing water
2 cups boiling water

Preheat the oven to 400°F. With an ice pick or skewer, pierce the softest eye of the coconut, drain the liquid, and reserve it for another use. (This is coconut water, not coconut milk, and makes a refreshing drink, as many on tours of plantations in the Caribbean have discovered.)

Bake the coconut for 15 minutes, then break it open with a hammer, and remove the flesh from the shell using the point of a strong knife. Peel off the brown membrane with a peeler and cut the coconut meat into small pieces. In a blender or food processor, grind the coconut in batches. When all the meat is ground, return it to the blender or food processor and, with the motor running, add the boiling water in a stream. Blend for 1 minute in a blender or 2 minutes in a food processor.

Allow the mixture to cool for at least 5 minutes, then strain it into a bowl through a fine sieve lined with a double thickness of rinsed and squeezed cheesecloth. Press hard on the coconut solids to extract as much liquid as possible. Bring the corners of the cheesecloth together and squeeze the remaining milk through the sieve into the bowl. Reserve the coconut crumbs for another use. Makes about 2 cups of coconut milk.

Festival

Traditionally served with fried fish at Hellshire Beach, this fried corn bread takes its name from the annual celebration held the first weekend in August to commemorate Jamaica's independence. It is terrific with many of the dishes in this book. ⏱⏱

1 cup yellow cornmeal
¾ cup all-purpose flour
¼ cup packed light brown sugar
1 teaspoon baking powder

¹/₂ teaspoon salt
1 egg
Water
About 2 cups vegetable oil for frying

Mix the dry ingredients in a medium-size bowl. Beat the egg lightly, then stir into the cornmeal mixture, adding enough water to form a stiff dough. Tear off pieces of the dough and roll into ovals in your hands. Heat several inches of oil in a heavy saucepan to 370°F. Gently drop a few dough ovals at a time in the hot oil. Fry until golden brown, then drain on paper towels. Serves 6.

Dumplings ⊘⊘

1 cup all-purpose flour
¹/₄ cup cornmeal
1 teaspoon sugar
1 teaspoon salt
¹/₂ teaspoon pepper
2 tablespoons unsalted butter

Sift together the dry ingredients and rub in the butter with your fingertips until the dough is crumbly. Add enough water to form a stiff dough, then form it into 1–2 inch oblong dumplings. Drop into hot water and cook until done, about 15 minutes. Drain. Makes about 20 dumplings.

Johnnycake ⊘⊘

2 cups all-purpose flour
1 tablespoon baking powder
¹/₂ teaspoon salt
1 teaspoon sugar
2 tablespoons vegetable shortening
About ¹/₂ cup water
Vegetable oil for deep frying

In a medium bowl, sift together the flour, baking powder, salt and sugar. Cut in the shortening until the mixture resembles cornmeal. Add enough water, a little at a time, to make a sticky dough. Knead the dough on a floured surface until smooth, adding additional flour if needed. Shape the dough into 2-inch balls. Heat the oil (use enough to cover the johnnycakes completely) in a medium-size skillet to 375°F. Fry the johnnycakes in batches until they are golden brown. Remove and drain on paper towels. Serves 6, 2 johnnycakes each.

Pie Crust ⊘⊘⊘

1/3 cup plus 1 tablespoon shortening
1 cup all-purpose flour
¹/₂ teaspoon salt
2–3 tablespoons cold water

Using your fingers or a pastry blender, combine the shortening, flour and salt in a medium bowl until the mixture resembles coarse meal. Add only enough water until the mixture forms a dough. Gather the dough into a ball. Dust with flour and cover with plastic wrap. Refrigerate for 30 minutes.

Roll out the ball on a lightly floured surface to an 11-inch circle. Place in a 9-inch pie pan and crimp the edge. To use as a prebaked crust, preheat the oven to 425°F and bake until golden brown, about 15 minutes. Be sure to use one of the two popular "blind baking" techniques for ensuring a fine baked crust, filling the unbaked crust before baking with either a pound of dried beans or one of those metal weights sold in specialty shops. Or fill unbaked crust with desired filling and bake according to recipe directions. Makes 1 crust.

ACKEE AND SALTFISH

Made with the fruit of a strange tree of West African origin, ackee and saltfish is considered the "national dish" of Jamaica. It is popular as part of a hearty Jamaican breakfast, or as an appetizer at lunch or dinner. Saltfish is any dried, salted fish, usually cod or mackerel. Ackees, which resemble scrambled eggs when cooked, are available fresh or canned on the island itself. Parts of ackee are toxic when the fruit is not perfectly ripe, so it is subject to import restrictions in some countries. If you prepare this dish with fresh ackee, it is important to choose ackees that are completely open, with the black seed and yellow fruit clearly visible in the scarlet pod. ☺☺☺

An island breakfast of (clockwise from right) Ackee and Saltfish, Johnnycakes (page 41) and Plantain Chips (page 48) on a table by Margaret Robson.

1 pound saltfish, boned
2 dozen ackee pods
6 bacon slices, cut up
1 Scotch bonnet or jalapeño pepper, seeded and sliced
2 scallions, chopped
1 medium onion, chopped
1 medium tomato, finely chopped
¹/₂ teaspoon freshly ground black pepper

Soak the saltfish in cold water for 30 minutes, then drain and place in a pot with 1 quart of water. Bring to a boil, then drain the water, and break the fish into flakes using a fork.

Remove the ackees from the pods. Discard the seeds and gently remove the pink membranes with a sharp knife. Parboil the pegs of ackee by covering them with salted water in a medium saucepan and bringing just to a boil. (The ackees will disintegrate if they are overcooked, so watch them carefully. Alternatively, you may want to cook them in a piece of cheesecloth tied with some string.) Remove the saucepan from the heat, drain the ackees and set them aside.

Fry the bacon in a large skillet until crisp, then reduce the heat to medium-low, and add the hot pepper, scallions and onion. Sauté until the onions are tender. Stir the ackees into the skillet, along with the flaked saltfish, tomatoes and black pepper. Cook over low heat 5 minutes.

Using a slotted spoon, spoon the saltfish mixture onto plates. Serve with boiled or pan-fried plantains and Johnnycakes (page 41). Serves 4.

STEAMED CALLALOO IN PHYLLO DOUGH

Everett Wilkerson, Grand Lido Sans Souci

As an example of what young chefs in Jamaica are doing today, here's an appetizer that uses the New World ingredients callaloo and ackee in a way that is reminiscent of Greek spanakopita. This dish is popular at the Sans Souci resort in Ocho Rios. ✪✪

2¼ **sticks unsalted butter, divided**
1 **small onion, minced**
½ **teaspoon minced garlic**
½ **Scotch bonnet or jalapeño pepper, seeded and minced**
¼ **teaspoon fresh thyme or dash of dried leaf thyme**
2 **pounds callaloo leaves, cleaned and chopped**
2 **medium tomatoes, diced**
Salt and freshly ground black pepper
10 **ounces mild cheddar cheese, shredded**
16 **phyllo dough sheets**
¼ **cup vegetable oil**

Sauce
1 **bay leaf**
10 **white peppercorns**
½ **cup dry white wine**
6 **cups heavy cream**
12 **ounces ackee, cooked, squeezed of all water, and pureed**

In a large skillet, melt 1 tablespoon of the butter over medium heat. Add the onion, garlic, Scotch bonnet and thyme and cook and stir until the onion is tender. Stir in the callaloo and the tomatoes. Cook for 5–7 minutes. Season with salt and black pepper to taste, and allow to cool. Stir in the cheese.

Brush the first sheet of phyllo lightly with vegetable oil and lay a second sheet over it. Oil the top sheet as well. Place one eighth of the callaloo mixture a quarter-inch in from the edge of the phyllo sheet along the length of the sheet. Fold in the long edge to cover the filling and then fold in the short ends of the sheet slightly, just so the filling is sealed inside. Then roll up the whole sheet so you have a cigar shape. Brush the top with a little more oil. Repeat with remaining phyllo sheets and filling.

To prepare the **sauce,** place the bay leaf and peppercorns in a heavy saucepan, cover with wine, and bring to a boil. Reduce the heat to medium-low and cook until the liquid is almost gone. Strain the reduced liquid and return to the saucepan. Add the heavy cream and simmer until liquid is reduced by two thirds. Add the ackee puree and simmer for 1 minute. Remove from the heat and whisk in the remaining butter, one tablespoon at a time. Season with additional salt and pepper.

Preheat the oven to 350°F. Place the phyllo packets, seam side down, on baking sheet. Bake until golden brown, about 10 minutes. Serve immediately with the ackee sauce. Serves 8.

STAMP AND GO

This dish, which gets my award for the most colorful name, is so called because Jamaicans love to snack on it during bus trips around the island. Picture a bus rider jumping down into the dirt, buying and swallowing one of these treats in one moment, then hopping back aboard as the bus pulls away—and you'll understand the name. It is often served with a spicy sauce like the Tomato-Scotch Bonnet one here. ☺ ☺ ☺

1/4 **pound saltfish**
6 **tablespoons boiling water**
1/2 **cup all-purpose flour**
3/4 **teaspoon baking powder**
1 **medium onion, finely chopped**
1 **garlic clove, finely chopped**
1 **tablespoon seeded and chopped Scotch**
   bonnet or jalapeño pepper
1 **tablespoon finely chopped fresh chives**
Salt and freshly ground black pepper
1/2 **teaspoon finely chopped fresh thyme or**
   dash of dried leaf thyme
2 **large eggs, separated**
Vegetable oil for deep frying
1 **teaspoon tarragon-flavored vinegar**

Tomato-Scotch Bonnet Sauce

10 **large ripe tomatoes, peeled and quartered**
3 **white onions, quartered**
1–4 **Scotch bonnet peppers, seeded**
3 **tablespoons brown sugar**
1 **tablespoon salt**
2 **cups malt vinegar**

To make the **Stamp and Go**, soak the codfish in water for several hours—it's best if soaked overnight. Drain. Pour the boiling water over the fish and let cool. Drain the codfish, reserving the water. Place the flour and baking powder in a large bowl. Gradually add the reserved water, stirring until well blended. Rinse the fish in fresh cold water. Remove any skin and bones, then break the fish into flakes using a fork.

Add the fish, onion, garlic, hot pepper, chives, salt, black pepper, thyme and egg yolks to the flour mixture, stirring until combined. Heat the oil to 350–375°F in a deep skillet. Beat the egg whites until stiff but not dry, then fold into the fish mixture along with the vinegar.

Drop the batter by tablespoons into the hot oil and fry until golden brown. Drain on paper towels.

To make the **sauce**, puree the vegetables in a food processor, then transfer them to a large saucepan and add the remaining ingredients. Cook the mixture over moderate heat, stirring occasionally, until it begins to boil. Lower the heat and simmer for 20 minutes more. Let the sauce cool and serve it with the Stamp and Go. You can bottle the remainder and keep it refrigerated. Serves 6.

FRITTERS, CHIPS AND SALSA

CONCH OR CODFISH FRITTERS

These island treats are popular in the Caribbean and the Florida Keys. Conch can be a real treat when it is carefully pounded to tenderize it before cooking. In this recipe, the conch is just finely chopped instead. To make codfish fritters, simply substitute saltfish that has been soaked overnight for the conch meat. ♨♨

$\frac{1}{2}$ pound conch meat
$\frac{1}{4}$ cup chopped green bell pepper
$\frac{1}{2}$ stalk celery, chopped
$\frac{1}{4}$ cup chopped onion
1 tablespoon tomato paste
1 tablespoon lemon juice
Ground red pepper
1 cup all-purpose flour
$\frac{1}{2}$ teaspoon baking powder
About $\frac{1}{2}$ cup cold water
Vegetable oil for deep frying
Cocktail sauce or salsa

Rinse the conch to remove any grit, then pat it dry and pass it through a grinder or food processor. Mix together the ground conch, bell pepper, celery and onion. Add the tomato paste, lemon juice and red pepper. Let stand for about 10 minutes, then stir in the flour and baking powder along with enough water to make a thick batter.

In a skillet, heat the oil until a spoonful of batter dropped into the oil rises to the surface (about 375°F). Place 2 tablespoonfuls of batter in the hot oil at a time, cooking until fritters are golden brown on all sides. Drain on paper towels.

Serve hot, 2 fritters per serving, with cocktail sauce or salsa for dipping. Serves 6.

PLANTAIN CHIPS

4 green plantains
2 cups oil
Salt

Peel the plaintains and slice them into $\frac{1}{4}$-inch chips. Heat the oil to 375°F and fry the chips for about 5 minutes, until they are golden brown. Remove the chips from the pan, drain them on paper towels, and dust them lightly with salt. Serves 6.

MANGO SALSA

1 large ripe mango, peeled, pitted and diced
$\frac{1}{4}$ cup minced red onion
1 Scotch bonnet pepper, seeded and minced
2 tablespoons lime juice
1 tablespoon fresh minced cilantro
$\frac{1}{4}$ teaspoon salt

Combine all the ingredients in a bowl and mix thoroughly. Refrigerate for 1 hour before serving. Makes 2 cups.

Mango Salsa complements the salty flavors of the Plantain Chips (left) and Conch and Codfish Fritters (right).

RED PEA SOUP WITH SPINNERS & COCO BREAD

Nigel Clarke and Clifton Wright, Grand Lido Negril

RED PEA SOUP WITH SPINNERS
🕐🕐🕐

Soup
- 1½ pounds beef
- ¾ pound pig's tail or ham
- 2 cups dried kidney beans
- 4 quarts water
- ½ pound potatoes (or yellow yams or cocos)
- 3 scallions
- 2 Scotch bonnet or jalapeño peppers
- 1 sprig of fresh thyme
- Salt

Spinners
- 1 cup all-purpose flour
- ¼ teaspoon salt
- Water

Soak the pig's tail or ham overnight in the refrigerator to remove excess salt. Cover the kidney beans with water and soak them overnight as well.

The next day, drain the beans. Drain the meat, cut it up, and place it in a soup pot along with the kidney beans and water. Bring to a boil, reduce the heat to low, and simmer until the beans are tender, about 1 hour. Add the potatoes, scallions, peppers, thyme and salt. Cook for 35–40 minutes more.

To make the **spinners**, combine the flour and salt in a small bowl. Add enough water to make a stiff dough. For each spinner, pinch off about 2 tablespoons of dough and shape into long, thin dumplings. Mix them into the soup during the last 15 minutes of cooking. Serves 6.

COCO BREAD 🕐🕐🕐

- 2 packages yeast
- 1 teaspoon sugar
- ¼ cup warm water
- ¾ cup warm milk
- 1½ teaspoons salt
- 1 egg, lightly beaten
- About 3 cups all-purpose flour
- ½ cup butter, melted

Dissolve the yeast along with the sugar in the water, then stir in the milk, salt and egg. Add half the flour and stir well, continuing to add flour until you have a dough that can be turned out of the bowl. Knead the dough for 10 minutes, until smooth but firm.

Oil a clean bowl and turn the dough in it until coated. Cover with a damp towel and let dough rise for 1 hour. Cut into 10 portions. Roll out each piece into a 6-inch diameter circle. Brush with melted butter then fold in half. Brush with more butter and fold in half again. Set the breads on an oiled baking sheet and let them rise until they double in bulk. Preheat the oven to 425°F and set a pan of hot water on the lowest oven rack. Bake the coco bread 12–15 minutes or until golden. Yields 10 large rolls.

PEPPERPOT

Terra Nova

This is the Caribbean's most famous soup—a hearty and sometimes peppery concoction that harks back to the first recipe swap between the Arawak Indians and their Spanish conquerors. The okra helps thicken the liquid in the African style, as it also does in the gumbo of New Orleans. ☻☻

2 pounds fresh kale
¹⁄₂ pound callaloo, or fresh spinach
20 pods fresh okra
¹⁄₄ pound salt pork, cut into thin strips
¹⁄₂ pound fresh lean pork, cubed
2 medium onions, thinly sliced
2 Scotch bonnet or jalapeño peppers, seeded and sliced
1 tablespoon chopped fresh thyme or 1 teaspoon dried leaf thyme
1 teaspoon ground cumin
Freshly ground black pepper to taste
6 cups Chicken Stock (page 39)
¹⁄₄ pound medium shrimp, in the shells, optional

Prepare the kale and callaloo by removing all of the stems, thoroughly washing the leaves, and chopping them coarsely. Chop the pods of okra.

Place the salt pork in a large kettle and sauté over medium heat for 10 minutes, rendering the fat. Discard all but 2 tablespoons of the fat, add the pork cubes and onions, and sauté until the onions are translucent, about 5 minutes.

Add the kale, callaloo, and all the remaining ingredients except the shrimp. Cover and simmer for 2 hours. About 5 minutes before serving, add the shrimp if desired and cook until the shrimp turn pink. Remove the salt pork just before serving. Serves 6–8.

Note: If you use spinach instead of callaloo it should only be added to the pot after the soup has simmered for 1¹⁄₂ hours.

The painted screen in the background by Inga Girvan Hunter is inspired by an actual Jamaican house in Port Antonio — complete with corrugated zinc walls, clothesline and ackee tree in the back yard.

GUNGO PEA SOUP

Winsome Warren, Jake's

That delicate slurping sound rising from Jamaica throughout the Christmas and New Year's holidays is nothing more than islanders finishing off the last drop of their Gungo Pea Soup. The peas of West African origin (also known as congo or pigeon peas) are traditionally eaten at this time of year. ✪✪✪

2 cups dried gungo peas
1 smoked ham hock
2 medium onions, coarsely chopped
2 carrots, coarsely chopped
1 celery stalk, with leaves
2 Scotch bonnet or jalapeño peppers, seeded and chopped
1 garlic clove, crushed
1 bay leaf
$1/2$ teaspoon crushed rosemary
$1/2$ pound smoked sausage, sliced
Dumplings (page 41)

Gungo Pea Soup (left) and Curry Pumpkin (page 127) on a table by Ritula Frankel.

Wash the peas and remove any grit, then place them in a medium bowl. Add enough water to cover the peas and soak them overnight. Drain the peas.

Pour 8 cups of water into a stockpot and add all of the remaining ingredients except the soaked peas and sausage. Bring to a boil, reduce the heat to low, and simmer for 45 minutes. Strain the broth, reserving the ham hock and discarding the vegetables. Skim the fat from the broth.

Return the broth and the ham hock to the stockpot along with the soaked peas. Simmer over low heat until the peas are tender, about 2 hours. Remove half of the peas from the soup with a slotted spoon, place in a food processor fitted with a steel blade, and process until pureed. Return the puree to the soup. Add the prepared dumplings and the smoked sausage slices to the soup and heat thoroughly. Serves 6–8.

Note: If the soup is too thick, add a little more water to it.

PUMPKIN SOUP & BAMMIE

Terra Nova

PUMPKIN SOUP

Jamaica's love affair with the pumpkin is consummated in this soup spiked with fresh ginger—another flavor that islanders can't seem to get enough of. ☺☺

2 pounds beef roast, cut into ¹/₂-inch chunks
4 quarts water
2 pounds pumpkin, chopped
1 pound yam, chopped
1 green bell pepper, seeded and chopped
2 scallions, chopped
1 garlic clove
1 sprig of fresh thyme
Salt and freshly ground black pepper
1 (¹/₂-inch) piece of fresh ginger, minced

Place the meat in a large soup pot, cover with the water, and bring to a boil. Reduce the heat to low and simmer uncovered until the meat is tender, about 1¹/₂ hours. Add all of the remaining ingredients except the ginger and continue to cook until the pumpkin and yam are tender, about 45 minutes. Remove the pumpkin and yam from the stock with a slotted spoon, place in a food processor, and process until smooth. Return the vegetable puree to the stock.

Season the soup with salt and pepper to taste. Sprinkle each serving with the minced ginger. Serves 8–10.

BAMMIE

This fried bread is made with ground cassava, which is available in West Indian and Hispanic markets. When a vendor shouts "Fry fish and bammie!" in your direction, you have just stumbled upon a fine, full meal. ☺

Vegetable Oil
3 cups ground cassava (yuca)
¹/₂ teaspoon salt
1³/₄–2¹/₄ cups water

Grease a medium-size skillet with a little vegetable oil. Mix the cassava and salt in a large bowl. Slowly stir in enough of the water to form a dough. Divide the dough into 6 equal pieces. Place 1 piece of the dough in the greased skillet. Keep the remaining dough pieces covered to prevent them from drying out. Press down on the dough in the skillet until the bammie is about 6 inches in diameter (Jamaicans often use the bottom of a floured bottle for this). Place the skillet over medium heat.

When steam starts to rise and the bammie's edge shrinks slightly from the side of the pan, press the mixture flat again and turn it over; this should occur after about 5 minutes. Cook another 5 minutes. Repeat with the remaining dough pieces, greasing the skillet as necessary. Serves 6.

OXTAIL AND BEANS

Norma Shirley, Norma at the Wharfhouse

The combination of broad beans (also called fava beans) and spinners makes this a super-hearty recipe with that extraordinary country flavor that Jamaican foods tend to possess. You can substitute beef or veal shanks if oxtail is hard to find. 🕐🕐🕐

2 pounds oxtail, jointed
$^1/_4$ cup vegetable oil
5 cups water
2 medium tomatoes, chopped
2 medium onions, chopped
3 garlic cloves, chopped
1 sprig of thyme
Salt and freshly ground black pepper
$^1/_2$ pound canned broad beans (or cooked fresh
　broad beans)
Spinners (page 50)

Wash and dry the oxtail pieces, then brown them in the oil in a large stockpot or soup kettle. Add 4 cups of the water and bring to a boil over high heat. Reduce the heat to low and simmer until the oxtail is tender, about 1 hour. Add all of the remaining ingredients except the beans and the spinners. Cook over medium heat, for 10 minutes, then add the remaining 1 cup water along with the beans and the spinners.

Reduce the heat to low, cover, and simmer until the liquid becomes a thick gravy, about 10 minutes. Serves 4.

ESCOVEITCHED FISH

Good Hope

This recipe is most likely based on the Spanish *escabèche,* in which fish is poached or fried and then marinated. This version is a simple but very tasty dish that is served with pickled condiments. When the fish is fried correctly the fins are deliciously crunchy. ☺☺

- ½ cup all-purpose flour
- 1 teaspoon freshly ground black pepper
- ½ teaspoon salt
- 6 small whole snapper or sea bream (3 pounds total)
- ¾ cup vegetable oil

Sauce

- 2 tablespoons vegetable oil
- 1 large Bermuda onion, peeled and thinly sliced
- 2 green bell peppers, sliced into thin rings
- 2 red bell peppers, sliced into thin rings
- 1 Scotch bonnet or jalapeño pepper, seeded and thinly sliced
- ½ tablespoon allspice berries
- ⅓ cup white wine vinegar

In a shallow bowl, mix together the flour, pepper, and salt. Dip the fish into the flour mixture, shake off any excess, and set the steaks aside.

In a medium skillet, heat ½ cup of oil over medium-high heat until very hot but not smoking. There should be enough oil to nearly cover the fish. Add the fish one or two at a time, and fry about 3–4 minutes per side, until they are golden brown. Drain on paper towels and arrange in a single layer on a large platter.

To make the **sauce**, wipe the skillet clean, reduce the heat to medium, and add 2 tablespoons oil, along with the onion, bell peppers, hot pepper and allspice berries. Stir-fry the vegetables quickly, about 2 minutes. Add the vinegar and cook 5 minutes more. Spoon the vegetable mixture over the fried fish, and serve the remaining sauce in a small bowl for dipping. Serve at room temperature. Serves 6.

Note: You can use mackerel, kingfish or tilefish for this recipe just as well. Substitute 6 (½-inch-thick) steaks (a total of 2 pounds) for whole fish if you prefer them.

RUN DOWN

Traditionally served with boiled green bananas and simple flour dumplings, or else baked breadfruit, this dish wears its heritage both in its name and in its ingredients. It is quick, it is easy, and it is made with the tropical flavors closest at hand. Here it is served with boiled breadfruit, a traditional accompaniment to meat, fish or poultry. ☺☺

3 tablespoons freshly squeezed lime juice
6 mackerel or other oily fish fillets (about 2 pounds)
3 cups Coconut Milk (page 40)
1 large onion, finely chopped
1 Scotch bonnet or jalapeño pepper, seeded and finely chopped
2 garlic cloves
1 pound tomatoes, peeled and chopped
1 tablespoon vinegar
1 teaspoon dried leaf thyme
Salt and freshly ground black pepper

Pour the lime juice over the fish fillets in a shallow bowl and set aside. In a heavy skillet, cook the coconut milk over medium heat until it turns oily, then add the onion, hot pepper and garlic and cook until tender, about 5 minutes. Stir in the tomatoes, vinegar and seasonings. Add the fish, cover, and cook until the fish flakes easily when tested with a fork, about 10 minutes. Serves 6.

Note: Breadfruit can be prepared any way that potatoes can: boiled, baked or fried. Boiled breadfruit is cooked just like potatoes. Start with unripe or green breadfruit, peel it, and boil it in salted water until just tender.

To bake breadfruit, preheat the oven to 350°F and place a mature breadfruit on a rack with a pan on the rack beneath it. Bake for two hours or until the skin gives a little when you press it. Once it has cooled enough to handle, peel and mash it with a little milk, butter and salt and pepper to taste. Baked breadfruit can then be fried or see the recipe on page 98.

Breadfruit can also be roasted on a gas grill. Roast it for about one hour, turning it often so that the skin is charred all over. When steam comes out of the stem end, the breadfruit is done. Remove the flesh from the charred skin and serve.

SCOTCH BONNET GRILLED FISH & PEPPER SHRIMP

Martin Maginley, Grand Lido Negril

SCOTCH BONNET GRILLED FISH

In the Caribbean, spicy grilled fish is very popular. Here a host of other flavors is given extra kick by the addition of Jamaica's beloved hot pepper—the Scotch bonnet pepper. ☺☺

1 teaspoon dried leaf tarragon
1 teaspoon dried leaf basil
1 teaspoon dried leaf thyme
1 teaspoon dried leaf oregano
1 teaspoon paprika
1 teaspoon fennel seed
1 teaspoon anise seed
2 cups vegetable oil
2 tablespoons freshly squeezed lemon juice
2 tablespoons freshly squeezed lime juice
2 tablespoons Worcestershire sauce
1 tablespoon dry white wine
1 Scotch bonnet or jalapeño pepper, seeded and finely chopped
6 small, whole white-fleshed fish (like snapper)

Preheat the grill. In a shallow bowl, combine all of the ingredients except the fish and mix well. Coat each fillet in the spice mix, turning to cover evenly. Cook on grill over medium coals, turning once, until the fish flakes easily when tested with a fork, about 15 minutes. Serves 6.

Note: Brushing a little vegetable oil on the grill before cooking could help stop the fish from sticking to the grill.

PEPPER SHRIMP

When you see bandannaed ladies on the side of the road selling bright orange things in clear little bags, this is what they're selling. Pepper shrimp are a favorite snack all along the coast of Jamaica. They can be very salty. ☺☺

1 cup vegetable oil
2 Scotch bonnet or jalapeño peppers, seeded and minced
2 garlic cloves, minced
2 teaspoons salt
5 pounds shrimp, in the shell
2 tablespoons vinegar

Heat the oil, peppers, garlic, and salt in a heavy Dutch oven. Add the shrimp and cook, stirring frequently, for 3 minutes. Sprinkle the shrimp with the vinegar and cook, stirring frequently, for 3 more minutes or until shrimp turn opaque. Serves 6–8.

Scotch Bonnet Grilled Fish (left) served with Festival (page 40) and Pepper Shrimp.

LOBSTER SANS SOUCI

Everett Wilkerson, Grand Lido Sans Souci

This recipe is a combination of several traditional Jamaican lobster dishes. The Jamaican lobster (see photo on page 10) is also called rock lobster. Its meat is firmer and stringier than that of Maine lobster. Rock lobster tails are available frozen. ✪✪

- 1 large carrot, chopped
- 1 medium onion, chopped
- 1 bay leaf
- 10 whole black peppercorns
- 4 cups water
- 1½ cups clarified butter
- 1 scallion, minced
- 2 teaspoons finely chopped lemongrass
- ½ teaspoon annatto seeds
- ½ teaspoon fresh thyme leaves
- ½ teaspoon minced garlic
- 1 eggplant, thinly sliced into rounds
- Salt and freshly ground black pepper
- 8 Caribbean rock lobster tails
- 1 cup whole kernel corn
- 1 Scotch bonnet or jalapeño pepper, seeded and minced
- ¼ cup grated coconut
- 1 cup heavy cream

Place the carrot, onion, bay leaf, peppercorns and water in a large pot and bring to a boil over medium-high heat. Reduce the heat to low and simmer until the carrots are tender, about 10 minutes. Strain the stock, discard the vegetables and bay leaf, and reserve the stock in the same pot.

In a medium skillet, add the clarified butter along with the scallion, lemongrass, annatto, thyme and garlic. Heat until hot. Remove from the heat.

Preheat a large skillet over medium-high heat. Coat the eggplant rounds with a half cup of the clarified butter mixture. Add the eggplant to the skillet in batches, and cook until tender. Remove from the skillet, season with salt and pepper to taste, and cover to keep warm.

Bring the reserved stock to a boil over medium-high heat. Add the lobster tails, reduce the heat to medium-low, and simmer until the meat is tender, 12–13 minutes. Remove the lobster from the stock and set aside.

Heat 1 tablespoon of the remaining butter, and quickly sauté the corn and the hot pepper for about 1 minute. Add the grated coconut and the cream, and cook until the liquid has become quite thick, 4–5 minutes. Season with salt and pepper to taste.

Serve the lobster tails with the remaining cup of butter on the side, along with the eggplant chips and the creamed corn. Serves 8.

SMOKED MARLIN SALAD

James Palmer, Strawberry Hill

Here's a dish you'll encounter often around Port Antonio, especially during the legendary autumn billfish (marlin) tournament. At that time, this sleepy north coast town is transformed into a reggae version of Hemingway's Pamplona. At least the marlin don't run through the streets! Strawberry Hill serves this salad with some tasty condiments.🕐🕐

*Island Gnocchi
(left, page 125)
and Smoked
Marlin Salad.*

**1 pound smoked marlin, thinly sliced
4 cups mixed salad greens, torn into bite-size
   pieces**

Guacamole

**1 large avocado
Juice of 1 lime
1 tomato, finely chopped
Flesh of 1 pineapple, finely chopped
1 onion, finely chopped
1 green sweet pepper, finely chopped
1/2 Scotch bonnet pepper, finely chopped**

Mango Salsa

**1 mango
1 Scotch bonnet pepper
1 cup white wine**

Pickled Onion

**2 large onions, thinly sliced
2 cups vinegar
1/8 teaspoon each allspice, cumin and thyme
1 bayleaf
1 tablespoon sugar**

Prepare the **guacamole** by pureeing the avocado and lime juice together. Add the remaining ingredients. Prepare the **salsa** by cooking the mango, Scotch bonnet, and wine together until soft, about 20 minutes. Prepare the **pickled onion** by cooking all the ingredients together over medium high heat, for about 30 minutes.

Place a small amount of the lettuce on each of 4 dinner plates, then drape the sliced marlin over the lettuce. Garnish with all three condiments. Serves 4.

BROWN STEW FISH AND TURN CORNMEAL

Thomas Swan, Grand Lido Negril

BROWN STEW FISH

Here is a very simple, old-fashioned recipe that islanders relish—even those who cook the fancy dishes in hotels and restaurants. ☯☯

- 6 fillets of mild white-fleshed fish (about 2 pounds total)
- All-purpose flour
- 3 tablespoons vegetable oil
- 2 medium onions, chopped
- 3 carrots, chopped
- ½ pound green beans, cut into thirds
- 2 scallions, chopped
- 2 tomatoes, chopped
- 3 tablespoons black soy sauce
- 1 quart Fish Stock (page 40) or water

Lightly dust the fish fillets with flour. Heat the oil in a large skillet over medium-high heat. Add the fish fillets and fry until golden brown on both sides, 5–8 minutes.

Remove the fillets from the skillet and drain most of the oil from the skillet. Add the onions, carrots, beans and scallions to the skillet and sauté until crisp-tender, about 5 minutes. Add the tomatoes, soy sauce and fish stock and simmer 8 minutes.

Return the fish to the sauce, cover, and simmer until heated through, about 10 minutes. Serves 6.

TURN CORNMEAL

You sometimes find this unusual corn bread served plain, but most often Jamaican cooks like to season it a little. In this recipe, it is seasoned well. ☯☯

- ¼ cup vegetable oil
- 1 large tomato, diced
- 1 large green bell pepper, diced
- 12 okras, sliced
- 1 large onion, diced
- 1 scallion, diced
- ½ teaspoon minced garlic
- Salt and freshly ground black pepper
- 1 quart water
- 2 cups yellow cornmeal

Heat the oil in a large saucepan over medium-high heat. Add all the vegetables and sauté them until they are tender. Add the salt, pepper and water and bring to a boil. Gradually whisk in the cornmeal. Reduce the heat to medium and stir vigorously for about 10 minutes. Once the mixture is smooth, cover and steam over low heat for about 30 minutes. Remove the mixture from the heat and let it cool slightly.

To shape the mixture into patties, divide the mixture into 6 small bowls and press the cornmeal down firmly. Turn the patties onto a plate and serve. Serves 6.

STEAMED FISH AND FISH TEA

Mark Cole, Grand Lido Sans Souci

In Jamaica, any nonalcoholic drink or broth is called *tea*. Here it is a flavorful fish broth that is used as a sauce for the fish. ☺ ☺ ☺

8 (8-ounce) whole fish (tilapia works well)
3 carrots, diced
1 large yellow onion, minced
1 (1–pound) head of cabbage, chopped finely
12 okra, cleaned and sliced
2 cho-chos, cleaned and diced
2 medium potatoes, cleaned and diced
1 small West Indian pumpkin, cleaned and diced
2 sprigs of fresh thyme
$1/_2$–1 Scotch bonnet or jalapeño peppers, seeded and minced
2 scallions, minced
1 teaspoon minced garlic
Salt and fresh ground black pepper
3 cups water

Fish Seasoning

1 medium tomato, diced
1 scallion, minced
1 sprig of fresh thyme
1 teaspoon minced garlic
$1/_2$ Scotch bonnet or jalapeño pepper, minced
$1/_4$ cup lime juice
Salt and freshly ground black pepper

Fillet the fish or have it done by the fishmonger, but be sure to keep the bones and heads.

Place the bones and heads in a soup pot, and cover with cold water. Bring to a boil over high heat, reduce the heat to low, and simmer, uncovered, for 10 minutes. Skim any impurities from the top, then add about one-third of the carrots and yellow onion. Simmer 20–25 minutes more. Strain the stock and discard the cooked vegetables and bones. Return the stock to the pot and bring the stock to a simmer.

Add the rest of the carrots and onions, cabbage, okra, cho-chos, potatoes, pumpkin, thyme, hot peppers, scallions and garlic to the stock and simmer 10 minutes, or until the vegetables are tender. Remove them from the stock with a slotted spoon. Season with salt and pepper to taste.

Meanwhile, combine all of the fish seasoning ingredients in a shallow dish, add the fish fillets, and turn over to evenly coat all sides.

Place the fillets on a work surface. Separate the vegetable mixture into 2 portions, reserving half for later. Distribute the remaining half of the vegetable mixture among the 8 fillets. Roll up the fillets and secure them with toothpicks.

Using a steamer, steam the fillets over the simmering stock until the fish flakes easily when tested with a fork, about 10 minutes. Remove the fish from the steamer and cover to keep warm. Drop the remaining vegetables into the fish tea to warm them.

Slice the fillets into rounds and serve with fish tea and vegetables. Serves 8.

ROASTED RED SNAPPER & SHRIMP SPANISH TOWN

Winsome Warren, Jake's

ROASTED RED SNAPPER ◐◐

4 (1½-pound) red snappers
½ cup lime juice
Salt and freshly ground black pepper
½ cup olive oil
1 large onion, thinly sliced
½ teaspoon fresh thyme leaves
½ teaspoon fresh oregano leaves
1 bay leaf, crumbled
1 medium onion, chopped
3 carrots, peeled and sliced
1 cup cleaned and chopped callaloo
2 garlic cloves, minced
1 Scotch bonnet or jalapeño pepper, seeded and chopped
1 tablespoon chopped fresh parsley

Rub the snappers inside and out with the lime juice, then season with the salt and pepper to taste. Pour 6 tablespoons of the olive oil into a large roasting pan or baking dish. Arrange the onion slices on the bottom of the pan and sprinkle with the thyme, oregano and bay leaf. Sprinkle with additional salt and pepper.

Drain the fish, reserving the lime juice; pour the reserved lime juice over the onions in the pan. Place the snapper on top. Quickly sauté all of the remaining ingredients in the remaining 2 tablespoons olive oil and place around the fish. Bake uncovered in a 400°F oven until the fish flakes easily when tested with a fork, about 30 minutes. Serves 6.

SHRIMP SPANISH TOWN ◐◐

4 tablespoons unsalted butter
1 large onion, finely chopped
1 green bell pepper, seeded and thinly sliced
1 or 2 Scotch bonnet or jalapeño peppers, seeded and chopped
1 garlic clove, minced
4 medium tomatoes, chopped
1 tablespoon lime juice
1 bay leaf
1 teaspoon finely chopped fresh parsley
½ teaspoon sugar
Salt and freshly ground black pepper
1 teaspoon Worcestershire sauce
1 teaspoon Pickapeppa sauce
1½ pounds peeled and deveined raw medium shrimp

Melt the butter in a large, heavy skillet, and add the onion, bell pepper, hot pepper and garlic, and sauté until the vegetables are tender but not browned, about 5 minutes. Add the tomatoes, lime juice, bay leaf, parsley and sugar. Season with the salt and pepper to taste. Simmer, uncovered, until the sauce is blended and slightly reduced.

Remove and discard the bay leaf. Stir in the Worcestershire sauce and Pickapeppa sauce along with the shrimp. Cook only until the shrimp have lost their translucent look, about 3 minutes. Serve with rice, if desired. Serves 6.

COCONUT SNAPPER WITH SAUTÉED CALLALOO

Terra Nova

Several classic threads of Caribbean food come to-gether in this dish—the Red Stripe beer, grated co-conut and callaloo are quintessential island flavors. ⊘⊘⊘

Snapper

    6 (5-ounce) snapper fillets, each cut into thirds
    Salt and freshly ground black pepper
    2 large eggs
    1³/₄ cups all-purpose flour
    ³/₄ cup Red Stripe beer
    1 tablespoon baking powder
    3 cups grated coconut
    ¹/₄ cup vegetable oil

Sautéed Callaloo

    2 pounds callaloo, Indian kale or spinach
    ¹/₂ cup butter
    Salt and freshly ground black pepper
    ¹/₂-1 Scotch bonnet pepper, sliced

Season the snapper fillets with salt and pepper. In a medium-size bowl, combine the eggs, 1¹/₄ cups of the flour, beer and baking powder; mix well. In a pie plate or shallow dish, pour the remaining ¹/₂ cup flour. Pour the coconut into another pie plate.

Dredge the snapper in the flour, shaking off any excess, then in the beer batter. Coat generously with the grated coconut. Heat the oil in a sauté pan until hot and gently slide the fish into it. Pan-fry the fish until golden brown on both sides. Do not allow it to burn. Drain on paper towels.

Meanwhile, prepare the **callaloo**. Wash the callaloo thoroughly in water, discarding any old leaves and tough stems. Chop into small pieces and cook in boiling water until tender; drain. Heat the butter in a large skillet. Add the well-drained callaloo and the sliced Scotch bonnet pepper and season with salt and pepper. Coat the vegetables thoroughly with the butter. Serve hot alongside the coconut snapper. Serves 6.

BLUE MOUNTAIN LAMB

James Palmer, Strawberry Hill

Here is a delightful rendition of lamb shanks, with a host of hot, bitter and sweet flavors direct from the island repertoire.🍪🍪🍪

6 small lamb shanks, trimmed
Salt and freshly ground black pepper
4 tablespoons unsalted butter
Grated peel of 2 oranges
Juice of 6 oranges
1 tablespoon vinegar
1 bay leaf
¹/₂ teaspoon angostura bitters
¹/₂ teaspoon Pickapeppa sauce
Chicken Stock (page 39), if necessary

The Maroons, runaway slaves who lived in the highest elevations of the Blue Mountains, ate variations of this jerk dish.

Rub the lamb shanks with desired amount of salt and pepper. Melt the butter in a heavy Dutch oven over medium-high heat. Add the lamb and cook until browned on all sides, about 10 minutes. Reduce the heat to low. Add all of the remaining ingredients, cover, and cook until the lamb is tender, about 1¹/₂ hours.

Remove the lamb shanks to a serving dish and cover to keep warm. Remove and discard the excess fat from the pan liquid. Bring the remaining liquid to a boil over high heat, reduce the heat to medium, and simmer until the liquid is reduced to about 2 cups. Add chicken stock to adjust consistency and flavor, if desired. Pour over the lamb shanks and serve with mashed potatoes, fried onions and fried plantains. Serves 6.

CURRIED GOAT & MANNISH WATER

Sydney Wilson, Grand Lido Negril

CURRIED GOAT

We have Jamaica's immigrants from India to thank for this incredibly addictive curry dish. ☺☺

2 tablespoons vegetable oil
1½ pounds goat meat, cut in 1-inch cubes
3 large onions, diced
2 garlic cloves, crushed
2 tablespoons Curry Powder (page 40)
2 large potatoes, diced
2 tomatoes, chopped
3 cups Chicken Stock (page 39)
1 tablespoon wine vinegar
Salt and ground red pepper
½ bay leaf
Cooked white rice

Clockwise from left: Mannish Water, Rice and Peas (page 92) and Curried Goat.

Heat the oil in a Dutch oven over medium heat, then brown the meat in batches. Remove the meat with a slotted spoon and cook the onions and garlic in the drippings until soft but not brown. Stir in the curry powder and potatoes and cook for about 3 minutes to release the curry flavor.

Add the tomatoes, stock, vinegar, salt and red pepper. Return the meat to the pan, cover, and slowly simmer for 1½ hours. Add ½ cup of water if the mixture is too dry. Add the bay leaf and cook 30 minutes more or until the meat is tender. Remove the bay leaf before serving over the rice. Serves 4.

MANNISH WATER

A "curry goat feed," a festive Jamaican get-together with curried goat as its main course, traditionally involves slaughtering a goat. Since parts of the goat aren't used in the curry, it has become custom to make this soup from those unused parts—the head and all of the organs. ☺☺

4 pounds goat head, organs and feet
3 gallons water
12 green bananas
2 pounds yam
3 cho-chos, chopped
1 pound coco, cubed
½ pound carrots, sliced
½ pound turnips, cubed
2 bunches scallions
3–4 Scotch bonnet or jalapeño peppers
4 sprigs of fresh thyme
Salt
Spinners (page 50)

Chop the meat into small pieces, wash, and place in a large stockpot. Add the water and bring to a boil. Reduce the heat to low and simmer until the meat is tender, about 3 hours. Add all of the remaining ingredients, except for the spinners, and cook until the vegetables are tender, 20–30 minutes, adding the spinners during the last 15 minutes of cooking. Serves 10–12.

BEEF TENDERLOIN WITH ACKEE AND CALLALOO

Martin Maginley, Grand Lido Negril

The Grand Lido in Negril takes the finest beef tenderloin and pairs it with rustic island ackee and callaloo—giving it a surprising Jamaican spin. Of course, these flavors work no matter what the eye appeal—but the resort likes to stack this dish for a dramatic appearance at the table.🕐🕐🕐

¼ cup olive oil
½ cup finely chopped onion
1 head of garlic, finely chopped
2 cups dry red wine
3 cups beef stock
Salt and freshly ground black pepper
2 tablespoons butter
12 ounces ackee
1 pound callaloo, cleaned and chopped
3 plantains
1 pound zucchini, sliced
1 pound carrots, peeled and sliced
1 pound cho-cho, sliced
1 pound yellow squash, sliced
2 pounds beef tenderloin, cut into 6 steaks
6 sprigs of fresh thyme

Pour half of the olive oil into a large saucepan. Add the onions and garlic and sauté until tender, about 5 minutes. Add a little of the red wine to the pan and continue to cook until the liquid is reduced. Add the beef stock and continue to cook until the stock is reduced to a syrup. Strain the stock through a fine sieve and season with the salt and pepper to taste. Whisk in 1 tablespoon of the butter. Keep warm.

Blanch the ackee in boiling water, drain, and set aside. Blanch the callaloo in boiling salted water, drain, and set aside. In a small skillet, heat the remaining olive oil over medium heat. Peel and slice the plantains, add to the skillet, and sauté until golden. Drain on paper towels.

Blanch all of the sliced vegetables in boiling water, then place in ice water to stop the cooking process. In a large skillet placed over high heat, sear the steaks on both sides and then place in a preheated 400°F oven to continue cooking to desired doneness. Remove the steaks from the oven and let stand 5 minutes before cutting each steak crosswise into 3 pieces.

Build the pyramid on a dinner plate starting with a slice of beef, then a layer of callaloo. Cover with another layer of beef, a layer of ackee, then the last slice of beef. Heat all of the blanched vegetables in the remaining butter in a large skillet, season with salt and pepper to taste, and arrange on the plate.

Set the plate in a hot oven for 2–3 minutes, then spoon on the warm sauce. Garnish with the fresh thyme sprigs and serve immediately. Serves 6.

JAMAICAN SUNDAY ROAST BEEF

Wayne Lemonious, Grand Lido Sans Souci

This is Sunday dinner in many households around the island. It can be served with pan-fried yams, lightly browned in butter or vegetable oil and sprinkled with salt. This roast is particularly beloved for its dark, rich gravy, given pungency by Scotch bonnet and Pickapeppa. You can simplify this recipe by buying a roast already tied by the butcher. ✆

1 boneless beef round rump roast (2½–3 pounds), tied
4 teaspoons salt
1 teaspoon freshly ground black pepper
1 sprig fresh thyme, minced
2 scallions, chopped
2 Scotch bonnet or jalapeño peppers, chopped
2 tablespoons minced garlic
2 tablespoons Pickapeppa sauce
2 tablespoons vegetable oil
Water

Take the tied roast, and make small cuts randomly over the surface. Combine the salt, black pepper, thyme, scallions, bonnet peppers, garlic and Pickapeppa. Fill the openings in the beef with the seasoning mixture. Cover the roast and refrigerate overnight to allow the flavors to blend.

Heat a Dutch oven, then add the oil and sear the beef on all sides. Add ½ cup of water and simmer, covered, adding small amounts of water throughout the cooking process. When the meat is fully cooked after 1½–2 hours, a fork should slide into it easily. Cut the strings and remove them before serving the roast with the pan juices. Serves 8–10.

SPICY SAUTÉED LIVER

Winsome Warren, Jake's

If you ever get bored with typical liver and onions, try this Jamaican version, which is a popular breakfast dish. It has a touch of fire from the combination of the Scotch bonnet peppers and the Pickapeppa sauce.🍲🍲🍲

 3 pounds calves' liver, cubed
 1 large onion, minced
 3 plum tomatoes, chopped
 3 scallions, chopped
 1 Scotch bonnet or jalapeño pepper, seeded
   and minced
 1 tablespoon minced garlic
 2 sprigs of fresh thyme
 2 tablespoons Pickapeppa sauce
 1 tablespoon dark soy sauce
 Salt and freshly ground black pepper
 $^1\!/_4$ cup vegetable oil
 $^1\!/_2$ cup dry red wine

In a glass dish, mix the liver with all the ingredients except the vegetable oil and wine. Cover and marinate in the refrigerator for 1 hour.

Heat the oil in a deep saucepan. Add the liver in batches and cook until browned. When all the liver is browned, return it to the pan, add the vegetables from the marinade, and cover the pan. Reduce the heat to low and simmer about 1 hour, adding the red wine about 20 minutes before the liver is done. Serves 6.

JERK PORK

Dave Parker, Grand Lido Sans Souci

Until recently, jerk pork was one unique dish. But with the world's embrace of things Caribbean, jerking became a universal cooking technique applied to chicken, fish, shrimp and just about anything else. ☺☺

⅓ cup allspice berries
7 scallions, chopped
3 Scotch bonnet or jalapeño peppers, chopped
3 garlic cloves
4 sprigs fresh thyme
5 fresh bay leaves
Salt and freshly ground black pepper
10 thick-cut pork loin chops

Prepare the jerk paste by heating the allspice berries in a small skillet over medium heat for 5 minutes, then pounding them until they are powdery. Add all the remaining ingredients except the pork, mashing them into a paste. Rinse the pork and pat it dry. Spread the paste over the meat, cover, and marinate for at least 1 hour or overnight in the refrigerator.

When ready to cook, preheat the grill to medium-hot. Push the coals to the sides of the grill and place the pork in the center, so that it is cooked by the indirect heat of the coals. Cook the pork for about 1 hour or until it is no longer pink in the center, turning it periodically so it cooks evenly. If desired, toss some additional allspice berries or bay leaves onto the coals to add more flavor to the smoke. Serves 10.

Note: As in the photograph, chicken and sausage can be jerked with great success using the same spice recipe and the same application technique as in this recipe. Some Jamaicans add the jerk paste while making their own sausage, but unless you're making them from scratch, you'll have to settle for spices on the outside only. Cook the chicken on the grill for 40–45 minutes, until its juices run clear. The sausage should cook for 20–30 minutes. To make a tasty **sauce** to accompany this dish, prepare the jerk marinade ingredients as in the above recipe, adding 3 tablespoons of grated ginger. Bring this to a boil with 3 cups of water. Dilute 3 tablespoons of cornstarch in a little warm water and add it to the sauce. Serve on the side.

ROASTED CORNISH HEN WITH THYME

Norma Shirley, Norma at the Wharfhouse

This elegant, island-flavored recipe comes to us from Norma Shirley, whose restaurant just outside Montego Bay is a draw for VIPs from around the world. ☻☻

2 Cornish hens
2 fresh limes, sliced
1 small onion
3 garlic cloves
1 teaspoon fresh thyme leaves
Salt and freshly ground black pepper
3 tablespoons corn or vegetable oil
1 tablespoon cane vinegar (or other vinegar)
1 teaspoon prepared mustard
A dash of lemon or lime juice
$\frac{1}{2}$ cup dry white wine
1 sweet potato, sliced and sautéed (optional)
8 large shallots, roasted (optional)
Fresh thyme sprigs

Rinse the Cornish hens under cold running water, pat dry, and rub them well with the lime slices. Rinse. Place the onion, garlic, thyme leaves, salt, pepper, oil, vinegar, mustard and lemon or lime juice in a blender and blend until the onion is minced. Rub the hens with the onion mixture, cover, and marinate in the refrigerator for at least 2 hours, preferably overnight.

Preheat oven to 400°F. Place the Cornish hens in a shallow baking dish and roast for 15 minutes. Reduce the heat to 350°F and roast until the juices run clear, about 20 minutes longer.

Deglaze the pan with the wine, stirring to create a sauce. Arrange the hens on a plate. Serve with the sweet potatoes, shallots and tropical fruits, if desired. Garnish with the thyme sprigs. Serves 2.

GINGER-TAMARIND CHICKEN & RICE AND PEAS

GINGER TAMARIND CHICKEN

It seems to have taken a long time for someone to think of combining two of Jamaica's most popular flavorings, ginger and tamarind. The tamarind nectar is available in Asian or West Indian markets in most parts of the world. ☺

5 pounds chicken pieces
Juice of 1 lemon or lime
¼ cup vegetable oil
3 garlic cloves, minced
2 medium onions, sliced
1 tablespoon grated ginger
2 cups tamarind nectar
1 cup water
Salt and freshly ground black pepper

Rub the chicken with the lemon or lime juice. Heat the oil in a Dutch oven over medium heat and lightly brown the pieces in batches. Remove the chicken, reduce the heat slightly, and add the garlic and onions. Cook until lightly colored. Stir in the ginger.

Pour in the tamarind nectar and water, then season with salt and black pepper. Return the chicken pieces to the pan, bring to a boil, cover, and reduce the heat. Simmer until the chicken is tender, about 1 hour. Serves 6–8.

RICE AND PEAS

This traditional dish is still called Coat of Arms around Jamaica, though the more generic name seems to be taking hold. It is probably Spanish in origin, harking back to the Moros y Cristianos (Moors and Christians). It is also served in Cuba, Puerto Rico and other Caribbean islands. This recipe appears in the photos on pages 81 and 89. ☺☺☺

1 cup dried kidney beans, soaked overnight
4 cups Coconut Milk (page 40)
1 garlic clove, minced
2 scallions, finely chopped
1 sprig fresh thyme, finely chopped or
  ½ teaspoon dried
3 cups uncooked rice
2½ cups water
2 teaspoons salt
1 tablespoon sugar

Drain the soaked beans and combine with the coconut milk in a medium saucepan. Cook, covered, over medium heat until the beans are tender but not mushy, about 1 hour. Add all the remaining ingredients. Cook, covered, over medium heat until the rice absorbs all the liquid, about 15 minutes. Serves 8–12.

Ginger-Tamarind Chicken served on Noel Coward's own plates at his beautiful home, Firefly.

FRICASSEED CHICKEN

Norma Shirley, Norma at the Wharfhouse

This is the typical Jamaican's favorite way to cook and eat chicken, though chicken fricassee recipes vary so much it's hard to call it one dish. Well, it is one dish—and here's an excellent rendition that should help explain its popularity. Rice is a nice accompaniment to chicken dishes. In Jamaica they cook rice with ½ –1 Scotch bonnet pepper for flavor and a little turmeric to give it a warm yellow color. ☯☯

1 chicken (about 3½ pounds), cut in serving
    pieces
1 tablespoon salt
1 teaspoon sugar
1 teaspoon black pepper
1 Scotch bonnet pepper, chopped
4 garlic cloves, crushed
3 scallions, finely chopped
2 sprigs fresh thyme
2 tablespoons vegetable oil
2 large onions, chopped
2 cups Chicken Stock (page 39) or water
1 tablespoon Pickapeppa sauce
1½ tablespoons tomato catsup
½ pound potatoes, peeled and chopped
¼ pound carrots, peeled and chopped
1 medium cho-cho, cleaned and chopped

Season the chicken with the salt, sugar, peppers, garlic, scallions and thyme. Heat the oil in a Dutch oven over medium heat and brown the chicken on both sides. Add the onions and sauté until they are lightly browned. Add the stock or water, Pickapeppa and catsup. Bring to a boil, then reduce the heat, cover, and cook for 15 minutes. Add the vegetables and simmer, uncovered, for 20 minutes or until the chicken and vegetables are tender, stirring occasionally. Serve hot with pan juices and with rice. Serves 4–6.

CHICKEN ROTI

James Palmer, Strawberry Hill

Here's a dish borrowed from the island's Indian population. Roti is a specific Indian bread that can be stuffed with an endless choice of curries. Here is one of the best.☺☺☺

Chicken Curry
1/4 cup vegetable oil
1 medium onion, chopped
4 garlic cloves, minced
1 Scotch bonnet or jalapeño pepper, seeded and chopped
1 (2–3 pound) chicken, cut up
6 tablespoons curry paste or 3 tablespoons Curry Powder (page 40)
4 cups water
Caribbean hot sauce or other hot sauce

Roti Bread
3 cups flour
3 tablespoons baking powder
1/2 teaspoon salt
1 cup water
Vegetable oil, as needed

Heat the oil in a large skillet over medium heat. Add the vegetables and sauté until tender, about 5 minutes, then add the chicken pieces. Add the curry paste and cook for 3 minutes, stirring occasionally. Add the water and the hot sauce to taste and stir. Reduce the heat to low, cover, and cook until the chicken is tender, about 45 minutes, uncovering the skillet for the last 15 minutes to allow the sauce to thicken.

Remove the chicken pieces from the skillet and cut the meat off the bone. Continue cooking the sauce until thickened, then return the meat to the skillet. Stir to heat the mixture through.

To prepare the roti bread, sift together the flour, baking powder, and salt, then add the water and mix to form a dough. Knead the dough until smooth and elastic, then let stand for 30 minutes. Knead the dough again and divide into 4 balls. Place the dough on a floured board and roll out as thin as possible, reaching a diameter of 8–10 inches.

Pour just enough oil into a large skillet to evenly cover the bottom of the skillet. Heat the oil over medium heat. Add the roti, cover, and cook about 1 1/2 minutes on each side, drizzling additional oil on each side as it cooks. Remove the roti carefully from the skillet and drain on paper towels.

Spoon the curried chicken onto the roti bread, roll up, and serve warm, accompanied by the hot sauce. Serves 6–8.

Note: Chicken Roti is served with slices of firm avocado, tomatoes and cucumber. In Jamaica they will often squeeze lime juice on top of the vegetables to bring out their flavors.

I-TAL FOUR-BEAN SALAD & I-TAL VEGETABLE STEW

James Palmer, Strawberry Hill

These easy and inexpensive recipes reflect the vegetarian cuisine of the Rastafarians in Jamaica.🍴🍴

I-TAL FOUR–BEAN SALAD

1 cup cooked broad beans
1 cup cooked or canned kidney beans
1 cup cooked or canned green beans
1 cup cooked or canned yellow (wax) beans
$^3/_4$ cup freshly squeezed lime juice
Fresh mint leaves

Mix the beans together in a large bowl. Pour the lime juice over the top and toss lightly to coat evenly. Cover and marinate in the refrigerator for at least 2 hours. Garnish with the mint leaves and serve. Serves 6.

I-TAL VEGETABLE STEW

2 large tomatoes, chopped
2 potatoes, peeled and cut into chunks
1 sweet potato, peeled and cut into chunks
3 medium carrots, peeled and sliced
2 medium onions, chopped
2 cups cleaned and chopped bok choy or callaloo
2 scallions, chopped
6 cups vegetable broth or water
1 teaspoon chopped fresh thyme

Place all of the vegetables in a large stockpot or soup kettle, then pour in the broth and add the thyme. Bring to a boil over high heat, then reduce heat to medium, and cook until the potatoes are tender, about 20 minutes. Serves 6.

SPINACH SALAD WITH BREADFRUIT CHIPS

Terra Nova

This combination of a tangy spinach salad with fried or baked breadfruit chips is a great way to kick off a Jamaican meal. You'll discover why breadfruit is an admirable substitute for potatoes. ◑◑◑

Spinach Salad

1 pound fresh spinach
1 teaspoon salt
6 scallions with tops, finely sliced
2 tablespoons lemon juice
2 tablespoons olive oil
Sautéed white onions, for garnish

Breadfruit Chips

1 green to semi-ripe breadfruit
Heavily salted water
Vegetable oil for frying

To prepare the salad, wash the spinach and discard any coarse stems. Drain and pat dry. Tear the spinach into large pieces and place in a large, shallow pan. Sprinkle with the salt and allow to stand for 15 minutes. Drain, squeeze dry, and place the leaves in a serving bowl. Add the scallions, lemon juice and olive oil. Toss lightly. Garnish with sautéed onions.

Peel the breadfruit, cut it into quarters, and remove the core. Slice lengthwise into thick wedges and soak for 1 hour in salted water. Pat dry with paper towels and fry, a few at a time, in 370°F oil until golden brown. Drain thoroughly. Salt lightly, if desired. Serves 6.

Note*: The breadfruit chips can also be baked. Follow the same soaking procedure and bake on a large baking sheet in a preheated 375°F oven until cooked through.

CALLALOO QUICHE

Good Hope

The delicious island green called callaloo provides just the right touch to turn this classic European dish into a Caribbean favorite. This dish is served with great success at the Good Hope Great House. For this recipe, cook the fresh callaloo just like spinach—blanch it briefly in boiling water with a pinch of salt.🕐🕐

4 ounces cheddar cheese
1 (9-inch) Pie Crust (page 40), unbaked
1 medium onion, chopped
1 tablespoon butter or margarine
3 large eggs, lightly beaten
2 cups milk
¾ pound cooked callaloo
2 Scotch bonnet or jalapeño peppers, seeded
   and chopped
½ teaspoon salt
A dash of freshly ground black pepper
1 red bell pepper, cut in strips

Preheat the oven to 425°F. Sprinkle half the cheese in the pie crust. In a small skillet, sauté the onion in the butter until tender, then stir in the eggs, milk, cooked callaloo, hot peppers, salt and pepper. Pour the mixture into the pie crust and sprinkle the remaining cheese over the top. Arrange the strips of red pepper on top. Bake for 30–35 minutes, or until a knife inserted in the center comes out clean. Serves 6–8.

OTAHEITI APPLES POACHED IN WINE

Norma Shirley, Norma at the Wharfhouse

This, of course, is a classic European dessert given a fling in the tropics at Norma Shirley's restaurant. The delicate flavor of the otaheiti, mixed with its tender flesh, takes on added character from the wine.②②

6 peeled otaheiti apples
3 cups water
1 cup dry red wine
1½ cups sugar
1 cinnamon stick
Rind of 1 lime
Rind of 1 orange

Coconut Cream
Coconut Milk (page 40)

To make the **coconut cream**, prepare the coconut milk as described on page 40, using 1 cup of cold water instead of 2 cups of boiling water. Set the coconut milk in the refrigerator overnight to allow the cream to rise to the surface. The next day, skim the cream from the milk and discard the remaining water.

To make the **otaheiti apples**, place the apples in a large saucepan. Add the remaining ingredients except the cream and bring to a boil over high heat. Reduce the heat to low and simmer until the flesh is cooked but firm, 8–10 minutes. (Do not overcook.) Remove the apples from the syrup and place in a large bowl. Continue to boil the syrup until it is reduced to a light syrup. Cool the syrup and pour it over the apples. Refrigerate and serve with the coconut cream. Serves 6.

Note: You can substitute canned coconut cream for the freshly made coconut cream.

PLANTAIN TARTS

Clifton Wright, Grand Lido Negril

Although plantains appear to be oversized bananas, they are usually served as a vegetable rather than as a fruit. Here they are sweetened and spiced, becoming a tasty tart filling. ☺☺

Pastry
1 cup vegetable shortening
2 cups all-purpose flour
1 teaspoon ground cinnamon
$\frac{1}{4}$ teaspoon freshly grated nutmeg
$\frac{1}{4}$ teaspoon salt
About 2 tablespoons ice water

Filling
1 cup mashed, very ripe plantains
$\frac{1}{2}$ cup sugar
1 tablespoon unsalted butter
$\frac{1}{2}$ teaspoon freshly grated nutmeg
1 teaspoon vanilla extract
1 tablespoon raisins

These fried pastry triangles (right) are Plantain Tarts. The Tie-a-Leaf (left, page 127) gets its shape from being cooked in a banana leaf.

To prepare the pastry, cut the shortening into 1 cup of the flour in a medium-size bowl until the mixture resembles peas. Add the remaining 1 cup flour, cinnamon, nutmeg and salt, then cut again until the mixture resembles bread crumbs. Add only enough of the ice water until the mixture forms a dough. Wrap the dough in plastic wrap and refrigerate for 1 hour or until firm.

In a medium-size saucepan, prepare the filling by combining the plantain, sugar and butter. Cook over medium heat until mixture is thoroughly blended and the butter is melted. Remove from the heat. Stir in the nutmeg, vanilla and raisins. Let the filling cool.

Preheat the oven to 450°F. Roll out the dough on a lightly floured board to $\frac{1}{8}$-inch thickness. Cut the dough into 4-inch circles and spoon about $1\frac{1}{2}$ teaspoons of the filling into the center of each. Fold the dough in half over the filling and seal by crimping the edges with a fork.

Place the tarts on a baking sheet. Prick the top of each with a fork and bake until pastry is delicately brown, about 15 minutes. Makes about 40 tarts.

BANANA LOAF & BANANA FRITTERS

Good Hope

BANANA LOAF

Desserts and breads have a close kinship in the Caribbean, where the latter often are served as the former. Breads such as this one blend the sweetness of ripe bananas with the crunchy texture of peanuts, making them either a fine ending for dinner or a tea-time treat. ☉☉

1/4 pound (1 stick) unsalted butter, softened
1/2 cup packed light brown sugar
3 large egg yolks
2 cups all-purpose flour
1 teaspoon ground cloves
1 tablespoon baking powder
1/8 teaspoon salt
2 very ripe bananas, mashed (1 cup)
1 teaspoon vanilla extract
1/2 cup chopped peanuts

Preheat the oven to 325°F. Grease a 9 x 5-inch loaf pan and set it aside. Beat the butter and sugar until fluffy in a medium bowl. Add the egg yolks and mix thoroughly. In a separate bowl, sift together the flour, cloves, baking powder and salt. Combine the mashed bananas and vanilla in a small bowl, then add this a little at a time to the egg-butter mixture, alternating with additions of the sifted dry ingredients. Beat the batter lightly until blended, then stir in the peanuts. Pour the batter into the prepared loaf pan. Bake for 1 hour or until a toothpick inserted in the center comes out clean.

Cool the loaf in the pan on a wire rack for 10 minutes. Remove the loaf from the pan and cool it completely on the rack before slicing. Serves 12.

BANANA FRITTERS

Few things could be quicker—or more delightfully sweet—than these fritters. Since bananas grow everywhere on the islands, Caribbean cooks are busy frying these fritters everywhere. ☉

1/3 cup all-purpose flour
1/2 teaspoon baking powder
Pinch of salt
4 ripe bananas, peeled
1 teaspoon lime juice
1 large egg
3 tablespoons granulated sugar
1/4 cup vegetable oil for frying
Powdered sugar

Combine the flour, baking powder and salt in a small bowl. Mash the bananas in a medium-size bowl and stir in the lime juice. Beat the egg and the granulated sugar in a large bowl; stir in the bananas, then the flour mixture. Heat the oil in a large skillet to 370°F. Gently drop the batter, a few heaping tablespoonsful at a time, in the hot oil. Fry the fritters until brown and crisp, then drain on paper towels. Sprinkle the fritters with powdered sugar before serving. Serves 6.

TROPICAL FRUIT MOUSSE & SWEET POTATO PONE

Dennis McIntosh, Ciboney

TROPICAL FRUIT MOUSSE

Almost any tropical fruit makes wonderful mousses —perfect for a light, refreshing dessert. In this recipe, both pineapple and mango are used for a delightful flavor combination.🕐

6 tablespoons cornstarch
1 cup unsweetened pineapple juice
1 cup mango nectar
$1/2$ cup sugar, or to taste
6 large egg whites
$1/8$ teaspoon salt

Two sweet island desserts— Tropical Fruit Mousse (left) and Sweet Potato Pone.

Dissolve the cornstarch in a bit of the pineapple juice. Pour the remaining juices into a large saucepan and sweeten to taste with the sugar. Stir in the dissolved cornstarch and bring to a boil. Boil gently, stirring constantly, for about 5 minutes, until the mixture thickens. Cool completely.

Beat the egg whites with the salt until soft peaks form. Gently fold the egg whites into the cooled juice mixture. Spoon into individual serving dishes or molds. Refrigerate until chilled. Serves 6.

SWEET POTATO PONE

Jamaicans never tire of anything made with sweet potato. This particular pone, similar to those found in the American South, was inspired by the rich culinary heritage of Africa.🕐

2 pounds sweet potatoes, peeled and sliced
2 teaspoons light brown sugar
$1/4$ cup butter
$1/3$ cup orange juice
2 large eggs, separated
$1/2$ cup dark rum
$1/4$ teaspoon salt

Cook the sweet potato slices in boiling water for 20 minutes or until tender. Drain them and mash with the brown sugar and butter. Stir in the orange juice. Lightly beat the egg yolks and add them to the mixture along with the rum.

Preheat the oven to 350°F. Grease a pie plate. Beat the egg whites with the salt until stiff but not dry. Gently fold the egg whites into the potato mixture. Pour into the prepared dish. Bake for 30 minutes or until a knife inserted in the center comes out clean. Serves 6–8.

GIZADAS & COCONUT DROPS

Clifton Wright, Grand Lido Negril

GIZADAS

Of all the sweet snacks in the Caribbean, this is one of the simplest and best. It's almost like a tiny tartlet, except that it's tossed together without the fuss of usual classic desserts. ☺

1 large coconut, grated
¹/₃ cup packed light brown sugar
¹/₂ teaspoon freshly grated nutmeg
1 recipe Pie Crust (page 41)

Preheat the oven to 375°F. Grease a cookie sheet. Combine the coconut, brown sugar and nutmeg in a medium-size bowl. Pinch off small pieces of the pie crust dough, and roll each piece out into a 3-inch diameter circle. Pinch up the edge of the circle to form a ridge, then fill with the coconut mixture. Set on the prepared cookie sheet. Bake until golden brown, about 20 minutes. Cool on a wire rack. Makes 6–8 servings.

These two coconut sweets, Gizadas (left) and Coconut Drops, are favorites with Jamaicans of all ages.

COCONUT DROPS

These delicious sweets are a combination of coconut, brown sugar and ginger. ☺☺☺

2 cups water
2 cups unsweetened flaked coconut
1 tablespoon finely grated ginger
2 cups brown sugar, packed
¹/₄ cup pecans or almonds, coarsely chopped

Butter a cookie sheet. Bring the water to a boil in a heavy saucepan and add the coconut and ginger. Reduce the heat to medium and cook the coconut for 15 minutes. Gradually add the sugar, stirring to dissolve it. Cook the mixture over high heat, stirring frequently, until it is thick and sticky (236°F on a candy thermometer), 20–30 minutes. To test for doneness, drop a little bit of the mixture into a glass of cold water. If it turns into a ball, it is done. Turn off the heat and stir in the nuts.

Using a teaspoon, drop the mixture onto the prepared baking sheet and let the candies cool. Makes about 20 large candies.

TOTOES & GINGERBREAD

Dennis McIntosh, Ciboney

TOTOES

If you'd like to introduce young children to the sweet tastes of the Caribbean, you might start where most island parents do—passing out these delightful snacks. ☉☉

2 cups all-purpose flour
2 teaspoons baking powder
1 teaspoon ground cinnamon
$1/2$ teaspoon ground nutmeg
$1/4$ cup unsalted butter, softened
$1/2$ cup granulated sugar
$1/2$ cup firmly packed light brown sugar
1 large egg, beaten
2 teaspoons vanilla extract
About $1/2$ cup milk

Preheat the oven to 375°F. Lightly grease an 8-inch round pan.

In a small bowl, combine the flour, baking powder, cinnamon and nutmeg.

In a large bowl, beat the butter with the sugars until fluffy. Add the egg and vanilla and blend well. Gradually stir in the dry ingredients, and enough of the milk to make a cookie dough consistency. Spread the batter into the prepared pan. Bake for 30–35 minutes or until golden brown. Let cool, then cut into 9 squares. (Leftovers store well in an airtight container.) Serves 9.

GINGERBREAD

The English, who first knew ginger from Asia, devoured gingerbread with particular passion in the West Indies. This gingerbread recipe owes its rich flavor to freshly grated Jamaica ginger. ☉

$1/2$ cup molasses
1 cup sugar
$1/2$ cup butter
$1/2$ cup hot water
2 cups all-purpose flour
2 teaspoons baking powder
$1/2$ teaspoon salt
1 teaspoon freshly grated nutmeg
2 teaspoons grated ginger
1 large egg, beaten

Preheat the oven to 300°F. Grease a 9-inch loaf pan, then line it with waxed paper. Gently heat the molasses, sugar and butter in a medium-sized saucepan over low heat, stirring until the butter is melted. Stir in the hot water and set the saucepan aside.

In a medium-size bowl, sift together the flour, baking powder, salt and nutmeg. Stir in the ginger and egg. Pour the molasses mixture into the flour mixture and mix well. Pour the batter into the prepared pan. Bake for 1 hour or until a toothpick inserted in the center comes out clean. Cool slightly on a wire rack. Cut in squares and serve warm. Serves 9.

Gingerbread (left), Totoes (center) and a large Gizada hiding in the corner (page 112).

TROPICAL FRUIT & VEGETABLE JUICES

Norma Shirley, Norma at the Wharfhouse

A selection of juices from Norma at the Wharfhouse. From left to right: Lime Leaf Tea, Pineapple-Ginger Drink, Jamaican Limeade, Fruit Punch, Tamarind Drink, Otaheiti Apple Drink, two glasses of Carrot Drink, Beet Drink and Soursop Drink.

FRUIT PUNCH ☉

Jamaicans use strawberry syrup to sweeten their fruit punch, but you can also add sugar to taste.

6 cups orange juice
2 cups pineapple juice
1 cup guava nectar
1–2 large mangoes, peeled and cut into chunks
2 small papayas, peeled and cut into chunks
Juice of 2 limes
3–4 ripe bananas, depending on their size
Strawberry syrup (optional)

Blend together all ingredients, pour over ice and serve garnished with fruit slices. Serves 10.

CARROT DRINK ☉

2 cups diced carrots
2 cups water
1 cup evaporated milk
7 tablespoons sugar
1/4 teaspoon grated nutmeg
1 teaspoon vanilla
4 cubes ice

Place the carrots and water in a blender and blend for 30 seconds. Strain the liquid and rinse the blender jar. Return the carrot juice to the blender along with the remaining ingredients and blend until thickened. Cover and refrigerate until well chilled and serve. Serves 6.

BEET DRINK ☉

2 cups water
1 cup diced beets
2 tablespoons condensed milk
1/4 teaspoon grated nutmeg
3 ice cubes

Combine the water and beets in a blender and blend until the beets are finely chopped. Strain the liquid, rinse the blender container, and return the beet juice to the blender along with all remaining ingredients. Blend 10 seconds. Cover and refrigerate until well chilled. Serve over crushed ice. Serves 4.

OTAHEITI APPLE DRINK ☉

1 cup sugar or to taste
1 quart water
1/2 ounce grated ginger
12 ripe otaheiti apples, chopped
Juice of 2 limes

In a large bowl, combine the sugar, water, ginger and apples and sprinkle them with lime juice. Place the mixture in a blender and blend thoroughly. Chill or serve over crushed ice with a slice of apple to garnish. Serves 8.

JAMAICAN LIMEADE ⏱

3 tablespoons sugar
1 pint water
Juice of 2 limes
Crushed ice

Combine the sugar and water in a pitcher, then add the lime juice. Stir and serve over crushed ice. Serves 2–3.

TAMARIND DRINK ⏱

4 cups shelled tamarind
8 cups water
Sugar
Crushed ice

Combine the tamarind and water and rub the mixture between your fingers to separate the fruit from the seeds. Strain the liquid and sweeten with sugar to taste. Cover and refrigerate until chilled. When ready to serve, stir in soda or tonic water if the chilled drink has become too thick. Serve over crushed ice. Serves 8.

Soursop, nutmeg (pictured with mace, the spice that grows as a membrane around the nutmeg seed) and limes are all ingredients in this Soursop Drink.

SOURSOP DRINK

Some Jamaicans call this drink Nerve Juice because it calms your nerves, but it is also a refreshing beverage that can be consumed at any time. You can leave out the condensed milk or, if you like, add a little sugar to sweeten the drink. Soursop leaves are also reputed to have healing properties and are used for sprains. ⏱

1 whole soursop
Juice of 1–2 limes, depending on the size of the soursop
2–3 cups water, depending on the size of the soursop
Condensed milk to taste
2 tablespoons white rum
Grated fresh nutmeg

Peel the soursop and place it in a bowl with the water. Rub the fruit between your fingers to separate the pulp from the seeds, then strain the liquid through a sieve to remove the seeds. Pour the juice into a blender with the remaining ingredients and blend until smooth. If the mixture looks too thick, add a little additional water. Serve over crushed ice and grate a little extra nutmeg on top to garnish. Serves 2–3.

PINEAPPLE-GINGER DRINK

This is a good way to use what's left over when you prepare a pineapple.☉

Peel of 1 fresh pineapple
1 (1-inch) piece of fresh ginger, grated
3 cups boiling water
Sugar
Crushed ice

Place the pineapple pieces in a large container with the fresh ginger, then add the boiling water and allow to set overnight. Strain the liquid, then sweeten with sugar to taste. Cover and refrigerate until chilled. Serve over crushed ice. Serves 4.

LIME LEAF TEA☉

This is a delicious after-dinner tea. It can be made with any citrus leaves—orange, lemon or grapefruit.

12–16 lime leaves
4 cups water

Wash the lime leaves in cold water. Bring the water to a boil, add the lime leaves, and simmer for 5–8 minutes. Strain the tea into a warm teapot and serve with slices of lime and sugar, if desired. Serves 4.

SORREL DRINK

Sorrel (also called roselle) is a tropical plant whose red petals are popular in drinks, jams and jellies. Though it is sold fresh in Jamaica at Christmastime, it is available dried all year. ☉☉☉

1 ounce dried sorrel petals
1 (3-inch) cinnamon stick
1 piece dried orange peel
6 whole cloves
2 cups sugar
2 quarts boiling water
$\frac{1}{2}$ cup medium dark rum
1 teaspoon ground cinnamon
$\frac{1}{4}$ teaspoon ground cloves

In a large heatproof jar or crock, combine the sorrel petals, cinnamon stick, orange peel, whole cloves and sugar. Pour in the boiling water. Cover loosely and steep at room temperature for 2–3 days.

Strain, then add the rum, ground cinnamon, and ground cloves. Cover and refrigerate for an additional 2 days. Strain through a fine sieve lined with cheesecloth. Serve in chilled glasses over ice cubes, if desired. Makes 2 quarts.

TROPICAL COOLERS

Grand Lido Negril

SIMPLE SYRUP

1 cup water
1 cup sugar

Combine equal portions of sugar and water in a heavy-bottomed saucepan and bring to a boil, stirring until the sugar dissolves. Cool and refrigerate until needed. Yields about 1 cup.

An array of tropical cocktails. Top row, from left to right: a Tropical Fruit Punch and a Yellow Bird. Middle row: Vodka Slush, Strawberry Daiquiri, Vodka Collins, white and red wine. Bottom row: Pink Lady and Caribbean Sky.

TROPICAL FRUIT PUNCH

2 ounces pineapple juice
2 ounces orange juice
2 ounces apple juice
2 ounces mango nectar
2 ounces strawberry syrup
1 cup ice cubes

Shake all the ingredients together with the ice cubes. Pour into 2 chilled glasses and serve. Serves 2.

YELLOW BIRD

2 tablespoons lime juice
4 teaspoons sugar
$2/3$ cup orange juice
$1/2$ ounce Tia Maria
2 ounces rum
$1/2$ ounce crème de banane
6 ounces Galliano
4 ice cubes

Blend all the ingredients in a blender and pour into a 12-ounce Collins glass. Garnish with tropical fruit. Serves 1.

VODKA SLUSH

$1^1/4$ cups lime juice
2 ounces Simple Syrup (recipe this page)
2 ounces Vodka
2 cups ice

Place all the ingredients in a blender and blend at high speed until slushy. Pour into 2 chilled glasses and serve. Serves 2.

STRAWBERRY DAIQUIRI

2 ounces strawberry syrup
2 ounces lime juice
2 ounces gold rum
2 cups ice

Place all the ingredients in a blender and blend at high speed until slushy. Pour into 2 chilled glasses and serve. Serves 2.

VODKA COLLINS

2 ounces vodka
2 ounces lime juice
2 ounces Simple Syrup
$\frac{1}{2}$ cup ice cubes
Club soda

Shake all the vodka, lime juice and simple syrup together with the ice cubes. Pour into 2 chilled glasses and top off each with club soda. Serves 2.

CARIBBEAN SKY

$1\frac{1}{2}$ ounces blue curaçao
2 slices of pineapple
2 ounces gold rum
2 ounces lime juice
2 ounces simple syrup
2 cups crushed ice

Place all the ingredients in a blender and blend at high speed until slushy. Pour into 2 chilled glasses and serve. Serves 2.

PINK LADY

4 ounces evaporated milk
2 ounces strawberry fruit syrup
2 ounces gin
4 ice cubes

Blend all the ingredients in a blender and strain into 2 glasses. Serve with short straws. Serves 2.

MANGO DAIQUIRI

4 ounces light rum
1 ounce curaçao
$\frac{1}{2}$ cup finely chopped fresh mango
2 tablespoons lime juice
1 tablespoon powdered sugar
2 cups finely crushed ice

Place all the ingredients in a blender and blend at high speed until slushy. Pour into 2 chilled glasses and serve. Serves 2.

Additional Recipes

SOLOMON GRUNDY

This exotic and flavorful starter is sometimes known as salmagundi, though it clearly harks back to British colonial days when herring from home was the favored postcard and Solomon Grundy was someone's proper name. Today, it's a fitting way to kick off an island meal. ①①①

$^3/_4$ **pound salt herring, or other salted fish**
$^1/_3$ **cup vinegar**
2 teaspoons minced onions
8 allspice berries
2 tablespoons vegetable oil
30 (1$^1/_2$-inch) bread rounds
Butter
Paprika
Chopped fresh parsley

Place the herring in a shallow dish. Add enough water to cover, and refrigerate for 8 hours. Drain the fish, cut into half-inch pieces and place in a medium-size bowl. Set aside.

In a small saucepan, combine the vinegar, onions, and allspice. Boil for 1 minute, remove from the heat, and add the oil. Pour over the fish. Cover and marinate in the refrigerator for 24 hours.

To serve, toast the bread rounds and spread with butter. Drain the fish and top each toast round with a piece of fish. Garnish with paprika and chopped parsley. Makes 30 appetizer servings.

MINCED LOBSTER

This is one of my all-time favorite Caribbean seafood recipes, borrowing elements from both the Spanish and the French Creole traditions. ①①①

3 (1-pound) lobsters, steamed
$^1/_2$ **cup vegetable oil**
$^1/_2$ **cup onion, chopped**
$^1/_2$ **cup green bell pepper, chopped**
$^1/_3$ **cup celery, chopped**
$^1/_4$ **cup bacon, diced**
$^1/_4$ **cup tomato paste**
4 large tomatoes, peeled, seeded and diced
1 Scotch bonnet or jalapeño pepper, seeded and finely chopped
$^1/_2$ **teaspoon fresh thyme leaves**
$^1/_2$ **teaspoon freshly ground black pepper**
Salt
1 tablespoon water
Cooked white rice

Remove the lobster meat from the shell and shred it by hand. In a medium skillet, heat the oil over medium-high heat. Add the onion, bell pepper, celery and bacon; sauté until the bacon is cooked and the vegetables are tender, about 5 minutes. Add the tomato paste, lobster and tomatoes and cook 5 minutes, stirring occasionally.

Stir in the hot pepper, thyme and black pepper, then season with salt to taste. Simmer about 3 minutes to reduce the liquid, and serve over the rice. Serves 6.

RED STRIPE CHICKEN
Winsome Warren, Jake's

Red Stripe brand beer, from Jamaica, has become popular all over the world. Connoisseurs order it for its distinctive blend of sweet and bitter flavors. Although any beer will work in this recipe, it deserves its name only when you pour on the Red Stripe. ☮

> ¼ cup vegetable oil
> 1 chicken (about 3 pounds), cut into serving pieces
> 2 cups coconut milk
> 1 cup Red Stripe beer
> 1 medium onion, chopped
> 1 large green bell pepper, chopped
> Salt and freshly ground black pepper

Heat the oil in a Dutch oven over medium heat and brown the chicken on both sides. Remove the chicken and pour off all but 2 tablespoons of the drippings. Return the chicken to the pan and add the coconut milk and the beer. Bring to a boil, then reduce the heat, cover and simmer until almost tender, about 30 minutes.

Add the onion and bell pepper, then season with salt and pepper. Simmer, uncovered, until the liquid has been reduced to a gravy, 15–20 minutes more. If the liquid evaporates before the chicken is done, add more beer. Serves 4–6.

SOY GINGER CHICKEN
Winsome Warren, Jake's

This delicious chicken recipe includes some of the most basic seasonings in today's Jamaican cuisine: soy sauce, ginger and brown sugar. ☮

> 3 pound chicken, cut into 8 pieces
> 1 large onion, diced
> 4 garlic cloves, finely chopped
> ½ cup soy sauce
> ½ green bell pepper, chopped
> ½ red bell pepper, chopped
> ½ cup cornstarch
> 1 tablespoon grated ginger
> 6 tablespoons brown sugar
> About 2½ cups Chicken Stock (page 39)

Clean the chicken. Place the pieces in a small baking pan and season them with onion, garlic and ¼ cup of the soy sauce. Add the green and red pepper to the pan. Cover the chicken with foil.

Heat the oven to 400°F and bake the chicken for 15 minutes. Remove the foil and continue baking until the chicken is lightly brown, about 15 minutes more.

Pour the pan juices into a bowl and mix in the remaining ¼ cup soy sauce, the cornstarch, ginger, brown sugar and add the chicken stock so that you have a total of 3 cups of liquid.

Pour this over the chicken and bake it for an additional 15 minutes, or until the juices run clear. Serves 4.

ISLAND GNOCCHI
James Palmer, Strawberry Hill

This being Jamaica, the gnocchi served here depart from the Italian original. Here they are made from sweet potatoes and dasheen, instead of the typical Irish potatoes. The sauce, however, is classic.
🕐🕐🕐

2 large dasheen
2 large sweet potatoes
3 eggs
$^1/_2$ cup all-purpose flour
1 teaspoon paprika
$^1/_2$ teaspoon ground cumin
Salt and black pepper to taste

Sauce

1 tablespoon olive oil
1 green bell pepper, roasted, peeled and
    chopped
1 teaspoon garlic, minced
2 teaspoons mixed herbs (thyme, basil,
    parsley, sage)
$^1/_4$ cup white wine
1 cup heavy cream
$^1/_4$ cup grated Parmesan cheese

Peel the dasheen and the sweet potatoes. Cook them in boiling salted water for 12–15 minutes, until they are just starting to turn soft. Drain. When they are cool enough to handle, grate the dasheen and sweet potato and allow to cool further. Mix in the remaining ingredients, using enough flour to form a sticky dough. Form the dough into small, oblong gnocchi. Prepare the sauce by sautéeing the pepper, garlic and herbs in the oil, then stirring in the white wine first, and then the cream. Thicken the sauce with the Parmesan cheese.

Bring 4 inches of salted water to a boil in a large pot and drop in the gnocchi. Simmer until they float (about 2 minutes), then remove them from the pot with a slotted spoon and drain them well. Set the gnocchi in the pan with the sauce and heat thoroughly. Serves 4.

PATTIES
Thomas Swan, Grand Lido Negril

Even Jamaicans admit that these spicy meat pies originated in Haiti—but no Jamaican worth his Red Stripe will let on that they're made better anywhere else on earth. The tinge of curry is a contribution of immigrants from India. Ⓙ Ⓙ Ⓙ

Pastry

2 cups all-purpose flour
$1\frac{1}{2}$ teaspoons Curry Powder (page 40) or good-quality commercial curry powder
$\frac{1}{2}$ teaspoon salt
$\frac{1}{2}$ cup vegetable shortening or margarine
Ice water

Filling

1 medium onion
2 scallions
1 Scotch bonnet or jalapeño pepper, seeds removed
$\frac{3}{4}$ pound ground beef
3 tablespoons vegetable oil
$\frac{3}{4}$ cup unseasoned dry bread crumbs
$\frac{1}{2}$ teaspoon dried thyme leaves
1 teaspoon Curry Powder
Salt and freshly ground black pepper
$\frac{1}{2}$ cup water

Prepare the patty **pastry** by sifting together the flour, $1\frac{1}{2}$ teaspoons curry powder and salt into a medium-size bowl, then cutting in the shortening with your fingers or a pastry blender until the mixture resembles coarse meal. Add only enough ice water to hold the dough together. Wrap in plastic wrap and refrigerate for at least 12 hours.

Prepare the **filling** by finely chopping the onion, scallions and hot pepper and mixing with the ground beef. Heat the oil in a skillet, add the meat mixture, and cook, stirring occasionally, until browned, about 10 minutes. Stir in the remaining ingredients. Cover and simmer 30 minutes, then allow to cool completely.

About 15 minutes before assembling the patties, remove the dough from the refrigerator and roll out to $\frac{1}{4}$-inch thickness on a lightly floured board. Using a 4-inch biscuit or cookie cutter, cut dough into 4-inch circles and sprinkle a bit of flour on each circle before stacking. Cover the stack with a damp cloth.

Preheat the oven to 400° F. Cover half of the first pastry circle with one twelfth of the meat filling, fold other half over, and seal by pressing edges together with a fork. Repeat with the remaining pastry and filling. Place patties on 2 baking sheets and bake until golden brown, about 30 minutes. Makes 12 patties.

CURRY PUMPKIN
Winsome Warren, Jake's

West Indian pumpkin has green skin and orange flesh. Its flavor is similar to that of the pumpkins found in the United States, but is really more like butternut, hubbard or acorn squash. If you want the flavor of the Scotch bonnet pepper without too much fire, simmer it whole with the vegetables, then take it out before serving. ☺☺☺

> 1 cup dried gungo peas
> 2 tablespoons vegetable oil
> 2 onions, diced
> 1 tablespoon curry powder
> 1 green bell peppers, sliced
> $\frac{1}{2}$ pound peeled and diced West Indian pumpkin
> 1 Scotch bonnet pepper, sliced (optional)

Wash the peas and remove any grit, then place them in a medium bowl. Add enough water to cover the peas and soak them overnight. Drain them, reserving the liquid.

Heat a heavy-bottomed pot for 2 minutes. Add the oil and onions, and sauté until the onions are translucent. Add the curry powder and cook for a few seconds, just until you can smell the curry cooking. Add the green bell peppers and the Scotch bonnet pepper and stir well, then add the pumpkin, peas, 2 cups of water and salt to taste. Simmer over low heat for 45 minutes or until the vegetables are tender. If the liquid dries up, add a little more if necessary. Serves 4 as a side dish.

TIE-A-LEAF
Clifton Wright, Grand Lido Negril

You'll find this intriguing marketplace sweet from West Africa sprinkled across the Caribbean. *Dokono* is the original Fanti tribe's name for it, though "blue drawers" seems to turn up pretty often as well. The name "Tie-a-Leaf" sounds the most Caribbean, since it's both poetic and intrinsically descriptive. You will need 8 banana leaves that have been boiled to make them pliable or 8 pieces of aluminum foil for this recipe. ☺☺

> 3 cups yellow cornmeal
> $\frac{1}{4}$ cup all-purpose flour
> 1 cup sugar
> $\frac{1}{2}$ cup grated coconut
> 1 teaspoon ground cinnamon
> 1 teaspoon ground allspice
> 1 teaspoon salt
> 1 tablespoon molasses
> 2 tablespoons vanilla extract
> $2\frac{1}{2}$ cups Coconut Milk (page 40)

In a large bowl, combine the cornmeal, flour, sugar, coconut, cinnamon, allspice and salt. In a medium-size bowl, mix the molasses, vanilla and coconut milk. Add this liquid to the dry ingredients, stirring briskly.

Place half-cup portions of the cornmeal mixture onto 8 prepared banana leaves or onto 8 squares of aluminum foil. Fold up the sides around the filling and tie each bundle together with banana bark or twine. Place the sweet parcels in enough boiling water to cover, and cook, uncovered, for 40 minutes, adding more water to the pot if necessary. Makes 8 servings.

Acknowledgments

On Location

All photos in this book were shot on location in Jamaica at the following hotels and restaurants:

Ciboney is in a spectacular tropical garden overlooking the sparkling waters of the Caribbean. The site, once a plantation and great house, offers a unique blend of privacy, amenities and incomparable service. In addition to 90 swimming pools, guests can enjoy authentic Jamaican cuisine in four restaurants. Main Street PO Box 728, Ocho Rios, St. Ann. Tel: (876) 974-1027.

Firefly was Noël Coward's home for much of the last 23 years of his life. Firefly is renowned for its views and history. Captain Henry Morgan used the spot as a look-out point, and while Noël Coward lived there he was visited by many top celebrities, including Sean Connery, Katharine Hepburn, Queen Elizabeth II and the Queen Mother. Firefly is maintained as it was when Coward lived there. PO Box 38, Port Maria, St. Mary.
Tel: (876) 997-7201.

Good Hope Plantation Great House (ca. 1755) looks out on a plantation filled with sugercane and groves of fruit trees and ackee. The rooms in the great house are decorated with period furniture, and the estate's spectacular gardens have resting areas where one can quietly enjoy the beauty of the surroundings. PO Box 50, Falmouth, Trelawny. Tel: (876) 954-3289.

The **Grand Lido Negril**, located on a secluded stretch of Bloody Bay beach, is the most luxurious resort in Negril and one of Jamaica's showpiece hotels. The hotel has three award-winning restaurants. Guests can go on glorious sunset cruises on the yacht on which Princess Grace of Monaco honeymooned.
Tel: (954) 925-0925.

Grand Lido Sans Souci, two miles east of Ocho Rios, fronts an expanse of private beach and blue Caribbean Sea. This resort offers all the conveniences and pleasures: gourmet dining, delightful cocktails, land and water sports, spa treatments and entertainment. PO Box 103, Ocho Rios. Tel: (876) 994-1206.

Jake's Village is a funky, colorful collection of cottages, a villa and an open-air restaurant and bar. Some of the cottages are actual early 20th century farmhouses made from wood and adobe. The pastels and earthtones of the buildings, the reed-roofed verandas and simple handmade furniture give Jake's a fanciful and unique feel. Treasure Beach PA, St. Elizabeth. Tel: (876) 965-0552.

Norma at the Wharfhouse, has received much critical acclaim from local and international press, and Norma Shirley, the chef and proprietor, was a guest chef at the James Beard Foundation International in 1995. The restaurant offers an eclectic and delicious menu served on the private deck, which has a magnificent view of the Montego Bay shoreline. Reading, St. James. Tel: (876) 979-2745.

Strawberry Hill is nestled on 26 acres in the picturesque Blue Mountains. The estate has gone through a series of incarnations. It was first a plantation with a great house, then a naval hospital. More recently, Bob Marley convalesced there after he was shot. In 1994 Strawberry Hill opened as an intimate hotel with a traditional 19th-century aesthetic. Irish Town PA, St. Andrew. Tel: (876) 944-8400.

The homey charm of the **Terra Nova** hotel, a former colonial great house, awaits travellers seeking comfort, convenience and personalized service in a cosmopolitan setting. The hotel is close to Kingston's commercial, shopping and entertainment centers. 17 Waterloo Road, Kingston 10. Tel: (876) 926-9334.

To obtain a list of stores that sell unusual Jamaican ingredients, please call the publisher at (800) 526-2778.

Sources

Pages 1 and 3: ceramic jerk vendor figurine by Orville Reid.

Page 4: sculpture from Living Wood; plate by Margaret McGhie.

Page 31: yabba pots and monkey jar from The Antiquarian and Trading Company.

Page 32: pot and wooden mortar and pestle from The Antiquarian and Trading Company.

Page 43: table painted by Margaret Robson.

Page 47: table painted by Margaret Robson.

Page 49: carved wood platter and ceramic bowl from Patoo Gallery.

Page 51: plates and bowl from The Craft Cottage; napkin from Patoo Gallery.

Page 53: soup bowl and carved chickens from Patoo Gallery; painted screen and clothesline by Inga Girvan Hunter.

Page 55: table painted by Ritula Frankel.

Page 57: calabash balls painted by Jasmine Thomas-Girvan.

Page 59: painted calabash candleholder, birdhouse and maracas and table mat from The Craft Cottage.

Page 61: ceramic platter and cup by David Pinto.

Page 63: parrot tray from Magic Kitchen.

Page 65: bowl from The Craft Cottage.

Page 69: hand-painted ceramic plates and bowl by Margaret McGhie.

Page 76: hand-painted ceramic plates and bowl by Margaret McGhie; wood carving and table from Living Wood.

Page 79: plate underlay from Strawberry Hill Gift Shop.

Page 81: wooden bowls and tray from The Craft Cottage.

Page 85: plates and bowls from Wassi Art.

Page 87: table painted by Ritula Frankel.

Page 89: bamboo salt and pepper shakers and jug from Living Wood.

Page 91: napkin from The Craft Cottage.

Page 93: table linens from Patoo Gallery.

Page 95: wooden rice bowls, salad servers and plates from Patoo Gallery.

Page 99: salad set from The Craft Cottage; bowl from Patoo Gallery; large wooden bowl and fabric from Strawberry Hill Gift Shop.

Page 101: leaf platter from The Craft Cottage.

Page 103: ceramic platter and wooden table and chairs by David Pinto.

Page 107: leaf platters from The Craft Cottage.

Page 109: ceramics by David Pinto.

Page 111: cake plate from The Craft Cottage.

Page 115: background painting and glass plates from Magic Kitchen.

Page 117: round wooden cake platter by Tony Barton of A. C. E. Woodwork.

Shops and Artists

A. C. E. Woodwork, which is owned by Tony Barton, uses hi-tech equipment—computers for designing the pieces and lasers to cut and engrave—to make items ranging from furniture to bowls, boxes and housewares. 14 Leonard Road, Kingston 10. Tel: (876) 929-3595.

Steve and Janine Solomon of **The Antiquarian and Trading Company** buy, sell, appraise and restore antiques. Their focus is on the products of Jamaican craftspeople and Jamaica-related items, such as early maps, books, prints and works of art that depict the island's history. 30 Hope Road, Kingston 10. Tel: (876) 926-658

The Craft Cottage is a unique gift store filled with ceramics, linens, paintings and many other charming souvenir items. The Village Plaza, 24 Constant Spring Road, Kingston 10.

The work of fiber artist **Ritula Frankel** reflects the richness of the Caribbean. Her hand-painted furniture, wall hangings, silk scarves and sarongs reflect the colors of Jamaica's plants and wildlife. Ritula's work can be purchased at the Nanny's Yard, an artist co-operative at Devon House in Kingston.

Fiona Godfrey works in a variety of media, including oils, acrylic and pen and ink. Her drawings appear in *Skywriting,* Air Jamaica's magazine. Her most recent works have been large-scale glass mosaics. PO Box 16, 23 deCarteret Road, Mandeville, Manchester.

Hi-Qo, in Kingston, sells old maps and prints.

Inga Girvan Hunter works in handmade paper and does print-making, drawing and painting. She also works with threads, feathers, bones, gold leaf and found objects. Her work is in many collections, including the Australian National Gallery and the American Craft Museum in New York.

Living Wood and **Magic Kitchen** are owned by Wolfgang Höhn. Magic Kitchen specializes in fine kitchenware, tableware and the finest in Jamaican handicrafts, sculptures and paintings. They also manufacture a full range of wicker furniture, baskets and mirrors. Living Wood carries a complete range of wicker furniture. Magic Kitchen, 24 Constant Spring Road, Kingston 10. Tel: (876) 926-6877. Living Wood, "Ocean Village," Ocho Rios, St. Ann. Tel: (876) 974-2601.

Margaret McGhie was born in British Honduras but grew up in Jamaica. She studied design and ceramics and has participated in art exhibitions in London, Trinidad and Jamaica. Since 1992 she has been producing hand-painted ceramic dinnerware and decorative objects that feature the colorful beauty of tropical fruit, flowers and foliage.

Patoo Gallery is an oasis for people seeking the best in Jamaican crafts. The store carries a wide range of textiles, carvings, tableware, linens, timeless Jamaican photographs by Cecil Ward, ceramics, Jamaican coffees, Busha Browne condiments and exclusively designed tableware. 184 Constant Spring Road, Manor Park Plaza, Kingston 8. Tel: (876) 924-1552.

David Pinto studied ceramics at the Rhode Island School of Design and refined his skills while working with artists in New York City. His pieces can be seen at his studio at the Good Hope Estate near Falmouth, and are part of the collection of the National Gallery of Jamaica. P.O. Box 700, Montego Bay 2. Fax (876) 979-8095.

Orville Reid's clay figures depict the unique and colorful life found along Jamaica's roads. Although he was trained in traditional pottery techniques, since 1979 Reid has been creating these hand-formed figures out of Jamaican clay. His work can be seen at **The Craft Cottage**.

Margaret Robson's work reflects the landscape, color and people of her native Jamaica. She is predominantly a muralist who uses large wooden cut-outs to achieve a layered, three-dimensional effect. She also specializes in the detailed decoration of furniture, such as the piece on pages 43 and 47, "Two Daughters." Her work is found in many private collections throughout Jamaica.

Jasmine Thomas-Girvan is a jewelry artist from Kingston. She is a graduate of Parsons School of Design and has held one-person exhibitions in Jamaica. She received the Prime Minister's Certificate of Excellence and a Commonwealth Arts and Crafts Award for 1997. Jasmine also designs and makes a variety of mixed-media craft objects.

Strawberry Hill Gift Shop is at Strawberry Hill.

Wassi Art sells wheel-thrown, hand-painted pottery with designs ranging from vibrant tropical flora to bold African patterns. These one-of-a-kind collectibles include bowls, plates, vases, sculptures and murals. Trinidad Terrace, New Kingston. Tel: (876) 906-5016. Prospect Plantation, St. Mary. Tel: (876) 994-1188.

The publisher would like to thank Andrew and Ashley Rousseau, who opened their home and hearts to us and helped us to discover the real Jamaica. Thanks are also due to Jasmine Thomas-Girvan and Norman Girvan for their enthusiasm and support; to Norma Shirley who shared with us her keen insights to the art of preparing traditional Jamaican dishes; to Susan Ward, Wolfgang Höhn and Christine E. Matalon who provided invaluable assistance in sourcing Jamaican artefacts, ceramics and handicrafts. Thanks also to Pat and Hertes Rousseau, Linda and Tony Gambrill, and to Donna Noble. Special thanks to Paula Summers, who came along for the ride and ended up being an indispensable member of the crew; to Mrs. Ong, for her gentle wisdom and humour; and a heartfelt thanks to the people of Jamaica for their unfailing patience and joie de vivre.

The publisher would especially like to thank all the hotels and their staffs who helped make this project a reality:

Ciboney
Earl Foster, General Manager; Marvin Thomas, Food and Beverage Manager; Dennis McIntosh, Executive Chef; Cleavie Thompson, Sous Chef; Michael Wilson, Pastry Chef.

Good Hope Plantation Great House
April Douglas; Lucille Hawkins; Myrtle Chambers, Chef; Denver Smith, Chef; Phillip Samuels, Chef; Patrick Small, Waiter; Clifton White, Waiter.

Grand Lido Negril
Rajiv Bhatnagar; Thomas Swan, Executive Chef; Martin Maginley, Executive Sous Chef; Nigel Clarke, Sous Chef; Sydney Wilson, Sous Chef; Clifton Wright, Pastry Chef; Vinroy Farguharson.

Firefly
Owen Mair, Director of Operations and staff.

Grand Lido Sans Souci
Patrick Drake, General Manager; Pierre Battaglia, Resident Manager; Everett Wilkinson, Executive Chef; William Eder, Executive Sous Chef; Linvil Green, Pastry Chef; Mark Cole, Sous Chef; Philip Woodbury, Chef Garde Manger; Wayne Lemonious, Supervisor; Dave Parker, Supervisor.

Jake's Village
Sally Henzell and Jason Henzell; Douglas Turner, Food and Beverage Manager; Winsome Warren, Chief Chef; Chris Bennett, Sous Chef; Angela Blake; Juliette Williams.

Norma at the Wharfhouse
Norma Shirley; Pauline Powell; Barbara Grey.

Strawberry Hill
Jonathan Surtees, Property Manager; Kyle Mais; Jenny Wood, Resident Manager; James Palmer, Executive Chef; Evol East, Sous Chef; Maria Anderson, Kitchen Helper.

Terra Nova
James Samuels, Chief Executive Officer; Gordon Edwards, Food and Beverage Manager; Patricia Kitson, Sales; Jackie Dixon, Front Desk; Alphanso McLean, Barbera Pottinger; Novia McDonald-Whyte; Maureen Graham.

Index

PERIPLUS WORLD COOKBOOKS

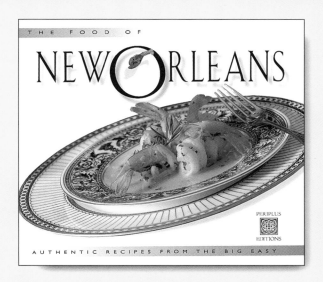

The Food of New Orleans
962-593-227-5

The Food of Santa Fe
962-593-229-1

All titles: 8³/₄" x 8" • 144 pages • $16.95

Please look for these books at your local bookstore or order from:

Charles E. Tuttle Co., Inc.
RR1 Box 231-5, North Clarendon, Vermont 05759-9700

Add shipping charge of $3.00 for the first book and $0.50 for each additional book
or call toll-free 1-800-526-2778 to order with your credit card.
Outside the U.S. dial 802-773-8930